Arguably, anyone can walk on water...

Outdoors, on a small lake, in Canada, in February

"Walking on Water"

for Debbie, Jared & Reece

who held my hand while I was walking, even when I was heading nowhere in particular... Thank you!

Some names have been changed to protect the innocent

D1520659

PROLOGUE

January 2020.

The year started like every other year, rather uneventful.

Some people had waited for their clocks to announce the arrival of the New Year. Some turned to the next page of their calendars in great anticipation of the dawning of a new year, a brighter future.

Sipping champagne. Hugging and kissing loved ones at midnight.

Many stayed awake to watch New Year's celebratory arrival shows on TV, streamed from across the world.

Fireworks at the Sydney Harbour Bridge. The ball drop at Times Square, New York City.

Basically, like the year before.

And the one before that…

Yet, many others just went to bed at their regular hour. Waking up, like every other day, but in a New Year. Their sleep interrupted by small-scale firework productions, by their neighbors. Around midnight, that previous night.

*****

I woke up early, as usual, on New Year's Day.

And *wealthy*.

I am always pleased to wake up. Especially when considering the alternative!

I do not mean *wealthy* like Bill Gates or Warren Buffet, but *rich*.

And for clarity, not *rich* like career politicians. But financially *okay*.

And by *okay*... I mean that, all things being equal - and based on my minimalist and generally thrifty lifestyle choices - I had squirreled away enough wealth to last the average person a few lifetimes.

I was financially secure. That is, secure enough to comfortably migrate into *early retirement* at the age of 51. That had been a few years prior.

Although, as I write this, I am more active in business now than before, albeit for different reasons, and with a different purpose, and mission.

Okay

Because imagining being *wealthy* is a relative concept.

If one were to be worth hundreds of thousands of dollars, but spending millions, that would not imply being wealthy. In such instance, a person would simply be living high, beyond their means.

But more about that later.

For the average person living paycheck-to-paycheck, it does not matter what the dollar number is at the bottom of their paystub. If they spend more than regular net income earned, received as reward for their work effort, they will always be poor.

Some people say that rich people invest their money, live as if they were poor, but keep investing.

Poor people, on the other hand, often spend as if they were rich. But they continue to live in relative poverty and never invest, or save, any money.

I do not understand a preoccupation to publicly display or make a show of wealth. Could it be that people who do this were once poor and then one day, somehow, got lucky?

Wealthy people often live seemingly average, boring lives.

Right among us, sometimes next door. Often without any obvious display of wealth.

In my humble experience garnered over more than five decades on this little planet, those who most visibly and ostentatiously display wealth are often least likely to have very much real wealth.

Some may even have been gifted great talent, like sporting or rock music superstars. But unfortunately, they may be hopelessly financially poor in real terms.

Or, heaven forbid, even financially illiterate.

We learned a little about a new virus during January 2020.

Several thousand people in Wuhan, China had suddenly become ill. People died. Great numbers of sick people recovered from this novel coronavirus. Or were infected, but asymptomatic.

The media mostly shared the aforesaid, not the latter, as is their custom. They are in the business of disseminating bad news... and this new virus was bad news!

Greed-fueled, imaginary cash registers started ringing.

Cha-ching!

The mainstream media would make bad news even worse. This is what they excel at and do in our ongoing, non-stop news cycle. Telling people what to believe, what to think, who to trust, and so on.

Fear mongering.

President Trump restricted travel from China to the United States.

Some opposition Democrats took to social media and television to share that they were outraged and offended.

"The President is a racist, xenophobe!", they tweeted and shared. They complained about the Administration's overreach.

Political miscreants are people from *the other side of the isle*, as both mainstream parties would typically suggest.

*****

By February, we were better informed about this novel coronavirus that was making people sick.

This new virus was spreading rapidly. It was a pandemic.

We learned about hot spots, like South Korea and Italy.

Soon, this would be coming our way, we were promised. There was a chance that millions of Americans might die. We were all encouraged to be scared. The country would need to close. The booming economy would need to grind to a halt.

A few radicals *celebrated* a potential American recession due to the pandemic. A recession would crush President Trump's chances of being reelected in November 2020.

Elation about the state of America's economic indicators showing any decline from its recent highs was astounding to most logical, rational people.

Celebrants seemed ignorant to the threat that they, themselves, might be joining the ranks of the soon to be unemployed. Of course, many felt they had nothing to lose anyway. The roaring bull market of the preceding few years had all but ignored many, passing them by.

President Trump had previously often used the booming Dow Jones Industrial Average ("the Dow") - an index of 30 large and successful American companies - as a personal Key Performance Indicator.

Or *KPI* for people who work for larger corporations or government institutions, where abbreviations are preferred because they serve as a type of insider language that outsiders would seldom comprehend.

The first instance of the novel coronavirus arrived in the United States.

The Dow started to decline.

A few Democrats deleted their *happy tweets* from the previous month, realizing that their social media utterances, combined with our impending doom, might not be perceived as *good optics* for their future reelection campaigns.

Criticism of President Trump was being replaced by a new narrative: he was now hopelessly unable and incapable of managing a war-like crisis that would grip, nay literally suffocate, all Americans.

There might have been elements of truth to this new narrative, especially since many trusted career bureaucrats were fabulously inefficient and unproductive anyway.

And President Trump happened to be the boss.

The CEO of the United States of America.

Their boss.

Many of the most vocal critics, including elected Congressmen and Women, had never held a real job before. Their personal experiences were limited to making appearances, ribbon-cuttings and delivering speeches. But this did not disqualify them from becoming loud, outspoken critics of the Administration, and its somewhat wobbly response to a growing, global pandemic.

Ordinary people started to stockpile toilet paper.

Psychologists sensed money-making opportunities. They could go onto cable news shows to explain why people were buying all the toilet paper.

In business terms, a shortage of toilet paper illustrates a fundamental macro problem with America's supply chain and related inventory management systems.

But no-one wanted to discuss business management and economic practices and strategies. These, as subjects, were not sensational enough to be deemed newsworthy.

We learned that the popular Just in Time ("JIT") inventory management strategy - meant to increase efficiency and decrease waste by receiving goods only as they are needed - might have some flaws.

On the positive side, JIT - as a strategy - reduced toilet paper inventory costs for supermarkets that ran out of supplies at the height of the pandemic. Of course, they also had to forego the commensurate revenue from toilet paper sales, along with potential additional impulse purchases of other goods.

There were no winners.

*****

I had a young lady working for me.

She had legally immigrated to the United States from Ecuador. Her family still lived there, in Quito.

At the office we talked about the coronavirus.

I mentioned a YouTube video that I had watched. The narrator said it had been shot in Ecuador.

He said people were dying and that mortuaries were overflowing. People did not know what to do with their dead family members.

I asked her if she had seen the video. She had not.

Then I asked her if she had inquired about her family. She said that she spoke with her mother daily, as before. She did not know exactly what I was talking about. I appeared to be more concerned about the coronavirus in Ecuador than my employee, originally from Ecuador!

A few minutes later she was back online, donating to a cause via GoFundMe. Her contribution was going to save koalas suffering and dying due to massive wildfires in southwestern Australia.

I was confused.

Or maybe, bemused?

*****

During March, the Dow became even more volatile.

Swings of more than a thousand points on one day became the norm.

Sometimes up, mostly down. More than ever before. Stock market losses started to mirror the Great Depression of 1929.

All over the world sporting events were cancelled. Churches, schools, and small businesses started closing.

These were not essential businesses. Supermarkets and gas stations stayed open. They were deemed essential.

Surely, "All businesses are essential?", people started wondering. Some dared to wonder out loud. All businesses support the livelihoods of the owners, employees who work there, and their families.

Local governments in oceanside towns closed their beaches to sunbathers and swimmers. It was safe to go to Walmart, but not safe to go to the beach?

Yes, people should rather go shopping. They would be safe inside a grocery store, where ventilation systems circulated a potentially lethal, air-borne virus.

But not on the golf course, or the beach.

People were told to practice social distancing. To wash their hands.

We were doing this *to flatten the curve*, they said.

Families started communicating via text, email, online Zoom calls, and social media.

Most supermarkets had bananas, but no toilet paper.

Some customers - who already had too much toilet paper at home - blankly stared at well-stocked produce sections, wondering when the supermarket would have more toilet paper for them to purchase again. This… and where or how the supermarket had managed to secure a full rack of bananas.

And they needed wet wipes, more Kleenex, and hand sanitizer. One day eggs would be sold out. The next, we were reminded to stock up on canned food.

Our actions resembled planning for natural disasters, like a hurricane. Except that this pending disaster seemingly lacked a predictable ending, like after a few days.

We were unsure what exactly to do, or what to expect.

We washed our hands with soap. But then we touched a door handle. So, we washed our hands again. For at least 20 seconds while singing, "Happy Birthday", to ensure that we invested the correct amount of time, cleansing our hands.

Supermarkets sold out of hand sanitizer. Soap was obviously useless.

The President and his Coronavirus Taskforce offered daily briefings. He was surrounded by highly skilled professional crisis managers.

We met Drs Fauci and Birx. They, along with other *experts*, offered specialist knowledge and instructions. Their instructions were deemed necessary information for *we, the people* to hear, follow, and abide by.

We learned about a requirement to *flatten the curve*.

"It would take two weeks", *experts* explained.

The Dow dropped even further. Still more. This was the worst stock market decline since 1931.

A guy on TV said so.

Some people wondered out loud, "Maybe they should just close the stock market down?"

*****

RUDI BESTER

MY STORY HAS THREE PARTS

PART ONE

POOR, HOMELESS & HUNGRY: A SURVIVAL GUIDE

Genesis - Chapter 9

PART TWO

"F.I.R.E."

FINANCIALLY INDEPENDENT, RETIRE EARLY

Chapter 10 - Epilogue

PART THREE

TIPS FROM THE INVESTMENT TRENCHES

Chapters 12-26

PART ONE

POOR, HOMELESS & HUNGRY: A SURVIVAL GUIDE

When I was young, I was very poor.

*Now, after a lifetime of hard work and commitment,
I am no longer young.*

GENESIS

My story begins at the time of my birth in Bellville, near Cape Town, in 1962.

This thriving coastal city is located near the southernmost tip of South Africa.

Being born in the early sixties means I am a *Junior* Baby Boomer. My Boomer peers were born between 1946 and 1964, for anyone wanting to keep score.

*****

I was born in the early hours of December 6th, 1962.

Basically, just a few minutes after midnight December 5th.

If I had been born a few minutes earlier, my birthday would have been on the same date as my older brother Sean. He was the youngest of my four siblings at the time of my birth.

Born into poverty.

Poor.

Although I was obviously unaware of this at the time of my birth.

I do not mean *poor* like people in America who consider themselves poor, because they work two jobs and they do not own their own motorcar.

And for clarity, also not *poor* like typical homeless people you see on the street.

But financially, we were not at all *okay*.

And by not at all okay... I mean that, we hardly owned anything. No home, car, furniture at home... but at least we seemed to have food to eat. I was fortunate in that regard because babies can be breastfed.

We were financially insecure.

That is, insecure enough not to know where the next meal would come from. Although, we did have some veggies growing in the back yard of our small, rented home. And there were a few chickens mulling about, mostly minding their own business, laying eggs daily.

Every so often, one chicken would have the misfortune of being identified as dinner protein. It was chased and caught by one of my older siblings, slaughtered, cooked, and consumed.

We were not okay.

But being *poor* is a relative concept.

My story strives to connect the dots between that day when I was born on December 6th, 1962, and the Prologue above, where I described myself as *wealthy*, in January 2020... some 58 years later.

CHAPTER 1

HOW TO BE HOMELESS WITHOUT KNOWING

My parents were poorly educated.

My mother was born in 1926.

I am not exactly sure of the year of my father's birth. Maybe 1920 or thereabouts. He was a few years older than my mother, as had been the social custom in the past.

Their birth years, respectively, were not great timing.

Albeit that this is something one obviously cannot control. The world was different then, at the dawning of the industrial revolution and in-between two World Wars.

Only people of extreme wealth or privileged backgrounds were well educated.

Most young adults of their generation did not finish high school.

As was common at the time for boys - although my siblings and I are not confident as to the exact timing - my father left school at an extraordinary young age.

He might only have completed the equivalent level of a Grade five or six education at various public schools he had attended.

This implies the acquisition of considerably basic literacy skills, at best.

For sure, he was able to read, write and complete basic arithmetic challenges.

But a healthy pre-World War II child from an underprivileged background with literacy skills was quickly co-opted into the workforce and encouraged to become a productive contributor, *to help feed the family.*

Times were tough at the turn of the previous century. Those tough times were exacerbated by uncontrolled childbirth and back-to-back, seemingly endless wars.

My mother fared only slightly better.

She might have completed a Grade 10 level education before leaving school. I am not certain. As far as I am aware, neither of my parents left any academic records for our review after their respective passing.

It was not uncommon for girls to leave school - *their families disgraced* - because of unexpected or unwanted pregnancies.

But my mother had birthed my oldest sibling in 1948. At that time, she would have been about 22 years of age.

My mother had therefore left school before completing a high school education for reasons unknown.

Common reasons might have included the expenses related to clothing, feeding, and supporting a young woman of *marrying age*. This cost would have been a heavy financial burden for a family of limited means, during the post-war period.

I have many blind spots related to my parents, their backgrounds, and their respective families.

My personal long-form birth certificate - issued in 1997 by the South African government's Department of Home Affairs - lists my parents' places of birth, and ages, respectively, but not their dates of birth.

At the time of my birth my father was about 41 years old. He was originally from Brakpan, a small town located about one hour east of Johannesburg.

I have no idea how my mother and father had initially found one another. Or how they met. They had been born and raised great distances apart from one another during a time of war, or shortly after the war.

My mother gave birth to me in 1962 at the relatively mature age of 37. She had been born and raised in Maitland, a suburb of Cape Town, located about midway between the city center and Bellville, my place of birth.

At least my family and I have government issued long-form birth certificates!

I found it at least a little amusing when President Obama - who had been born into a more affluent, modern, and more developed country in 1961 - appeared somewhat challenged when called upon to provide his long-form birth certificate.

The Canadian High Commission had requested our long form birth certificates for immigration purposes, in 1997.

I paid a relatively small tax and received the handwritten documents a few days later.

Are we to conclude that birth registry and related recordkeeping services in the State of Hawaii were less sophisticated than that of their peers in the Republic of South Africa - a so-called developing nation - circa 1961-1962?

*****

But I digress…

One day, when I was almost 5 years old, my father left my mother and my four siblings to fend for ourselves. My father did not experience some unfortunate life event, like dying unexpectedly.

He just left and never returned.

My mother was immediately, suddenly, a single mother with five children.

A few years later, my mother would die when I was 12 years old, just before my 13th birthday. Because of these events, I have childhood memory gaps that can only be filled anecdotally, for example by my older siblings.

But childhood stories, like enduring myths, evolve over time.

For the purposes of this story, the recollections shared are all my own memories.

My siblings are older than me. But their family history data repositories are also sometimes a little sketchy and occasionally, contradict mine.

Anyway, dates are not material to my story, save for the purposes of providing a backdrop to my past. And to help illustrate the shaky family foundation that I had been born into.

*****

It was late 2019.

Together with my wife and our younger son, we had watched a newly-released Indie movie called *"Unwelcome. Homeless in The Shadow of The Sun".*

The title adequately describes the topic of the film.

During the movie they featured a young, homeless woman. The interviewer asked her, "Where did you live while you were homeless?"

She explained that she would couch-surf. And that she would move between family and friends. Staying with someone for a few days, then moving in (or visiting) someone else for a while, staying in a hotel, and so on.

The movie had a profound effect on me, but perhaps not for reasons you might imagine.

When we left the theater, on our way to the car, I shared information with my family that I had never shared with anyone before: "I am 57 years old. Tonight, for the first time, I realized that I had been homeless for nearly a third of my life."

It is difficult to define homelessness to someone who might be oblivious to another person's plight in this regard. Generally, we view homelessness through the lens of our observations of people who are *living on the street*, or *sleeping hard*, as some people in the UK say.

But homelessness includes invisible masses. These masses include proud folk who are better at dealing with or hiding their homelessness, than the more visible *street people*.

Not all homeless people live in makeshift shelters under a bridge or overpass.

The term *homeless* should include all people who do not have a home to go to for rest, shelter, and relative comfort, at the end of their day.

Homelessness is a situational state of being, rather than an observable place like a temporary shelter on a sidewalk.

*****

My awakening began at the age of 5, when my father left our family.

He literally just disappeared. I was old enough to realize something was amiss.

My father was gone.

In a way I was relieved, because he used to abuse us mentally and hurt us physically. Like weak men who pretend to be tough often do.

All of us, including my mother.

His wife.

We were living in a small house where we had been for a short while, perhaps only for a few months. We did not own the house and we were likely facing eviction for not paying the monthly rent.

We moved frequently.

Our furnishings were sparse. It included a few pieces that had been left in the house by the owner or previous tenant.

My mother was now a single mother with a limited education, hardly any work experience, no savings, and no earthly possessions other than some personal effects and clothing.

A woman and four children.

Left destitute.

This creates a foundation for a state of perpetual under-performance, life-long poverty, limited opportunities for achievement or even future aspirations!

But my mother refused to teach her children to become victims.

She never appropriated blame.

She did not look back. She looked ahead. She would rather be a survivor. And drag us all along, albeit while figuratively kicking and screaming.

She had four children to feed. Four, because the oldest sibling - my brother Gerald - had been conscripted and called up for 9 months of mandatory military service.

Viewed objectively, military service implies free board and lodging, clothing, and meals.

You see, it is possible to view almost any situation with optimistic positivity when given a little time to consider the facts of the matter.

*****

My maternal grandmother lived in East London, more than 600 miles from Cape Town.

She very kindly offered to accommodate us.

For a while anyway.

We were excited about relocating and traveling to East London.

We - the kids - called her Ouma.

Her husband had died a few years prior. Ouma lived in a humble home she had previously shared with her husband.

He had worked for the South African Railways for his entire adult life. One employer for life, as was the custom those days.

With some financial assistance from Ouma we were soon all aboard a train… destiny, East London.

Our travel time was two full days and one night, spent in a *sleeper compartment* on a train.

We had no idea that commuting by train would be so incredibly tedious and boring. And anyway, how many card games can one play while being incarcerated with family members in a small holding cell, of a slow-moving train?

We carried all our possessions by hand. These consisted of a few bags and suitcases. Our personal possessions were mainly items of clothing.

Ouma was a licensed driver. This was quite unusual for a woman at the time. And she owned a car. A white VW Beetle. The car was in good running condition, and well maintained. It had probably not been driven much since her husband died.

She picked us up at the station in East London.

We scattered throughout Ouma's house for rooming purposes, as instructed.

Generosity is welcomed when one needs respite!

Simple things. A cup of soup with a slice of bread. A soft pillow to lay one's head when weary.

Sometimes one's immediate savior is a little old lady... witty, funny, with a sneaky, sarcastic smile.

*****

I was about to turn 6, and legally required to enroll and start elementary school.

The challenges my mother faced were extraordinary.

She had to learn basic project and logistics management hands-on, urgently, with little or no room for error.

In a commercial enterprise, my mother - if she were to have been afforded an opportunity to engage in a meaningful manner - would have been an exceptional employee and contributor.

She was a quick study, capable of making good decisions on the fly, and able to execute fearlessly!

My mother now had three young boys to tend to. She had to enroll us at schools, arrange transport of sorts between home and school, purchase school uniforms (required at the time), equip us with supplies, etc.

Oh, and then she had to find an ongoing source of regular income.

She scanned newspapers for jobs, networked and searched for any jobs that she might be able to do. She applied at many businesses, in person, as was customary during that time. She simply had to secure gainful employment and earn a regular income... despite her humble background, extremely limited skillset, and lack of relevant work experience.

My sister was 16 at the time. Old enough to leave school and find a job, or a husband, or something. One must do whatever one has to do to survive.

Once my mother managed to find work we were quite settled.

For more than three years I attended just one school. For children who are homeless, attending school offers some respite from a homelife that is generally undesirable.

To this end, I loved school!

My one-way bus fare was 3 cents. When we did not have any money, or on occasion when I had lost or misplaced my bus fare, I simply walked between home and school, some 2 miles. I did not dare to tell anyone, mainly for fear of being punished.

And of course, the walk was uphill, both ways!

*****

As you might guess... mothers and daughters - especially when both are older, mature, have families of their own, and so on - do not necessarily cohabitate on good terms for indefinite periods.

It would be bold for me to accuse Ouma of kicking us to the curb. But we moved on because it was time, and for reasons one can only imagine.

My mother earned a meager income. But she calculated that one hotel room - rented on a month-to-month basis - was within her financial affordability range.

In her hierarchy of servicing her expenses, rent would be paid after she had paid her tithes to the church.

She would often remind us to *Give to Caesar what belongs to Caesar.*

God would take care of everything else.

He never did.

Joe Hill wrote these words in "The Preacher and the Slave" in 1911:

> *Work and pray, live on hay*
> *You'll get pie in the sky when you die.*

My mother probably did not know about this song.

Yet, like many, she would frequently use the term *pie in the sky* for anything that resembled an unattainable dream, a great aspiration, or pretty much anything that seemed beyond her financial reach.

Effectively, after servicing her primary two accounts payable - tithes and rent; in that order - my mother would basically be *flat broke* mere days after her last payday.

Of course, from that date and until the next payday, the four of us needed basic sustenance.

Food was scarce!

My mother detested any form of debt. Fortunately, credit cards did not yet exist, otherwise she might well have been in debt instead of just broke.

*****

Now, before you have illusions of us moving into the Ritz Carlton Hotel as permanent residents, I shall briefly explain our version of a rented hotel room.

Residential hotels were common when I was a child. They might still be common today, but I am out of touch and simply do not know for sure. Sometimes I drive by motels that advertise rooms at *low monthly rates* on roadside signs, but I never really pay much attention.

These residential hotels are, and were, usually located in less desirable residential or city areas.

For reasons related to the typical target renter audience - financially desperate, lower-income residents - monthly rates were often reasonable and commensurate with a lack of equipment, fixtures, fittings, and services (usually none).

So, there we were in our grand new residence.

My mother and three young boys sharing one hotel room with four small beds. We would call the beds, a small table and its four rickety chairs, *our furniture*.

Mother taught her boys some manners. Like asking us to leave the room, or at least turn to face the wall while she was getting dressed.

She called it, *etiquette*.

She would often start a sentence with, "etiquette says…".

One of my brothers still sometimes jokes today about *this guy called Etiquette* who was always saying stuff.

And my mother had rules. She insisted that I should be asleep by the time she returned from a prayer meeting at her church on a Wednesday evening. I never was, and I also never learned to fake sleep properly.

We shared communal bathroom facilities with other residents. Bathrooms were located down the hallway.

We had comfortable beds to sleep in and restroom facilities with clean, running water. Residents provided their own supplies - soap, shampoo, and towels - when using the shared bathroom facilities.

We were doing relatively fine. And my mother reminded us that there were always people less fortunate. This is true regardless of where you might find yourself, and your circumstances at that time.

"You are not allowed to be dirty just because we are poor", my mother would say.

My brothers and I bathed at least every other day, sometimes once a week… unless no-one happened to pay attention.

When we ran out of toothpaste, we used table salt. We did not know any better. At least we would still clean our teeth.

Hotel staff sometimes took pity on us. The kids anyway.

Often, when they would see us hanging around the hotel kitchen, they would give us some food. A bowl or rice or porridge. Occasionally with some sauce. Sometimes even with a few cuts of meat if leftovers were available.

My brothers and I learned to fish. To be fair, my two older brothers learned to fish, and I would watch. They would allocate me small tasks like cutting bait, unravelling knotted fishing lines, or cleaning fish that we had caught.

I was seven years old and learning the phrase, *give a man a fish and you feed him for a day. Teach him to fish…*

It was a lesson in sustainability and self-sufficiency.

It was also an introduction to capitalism because we learned to barter, trade, and do menial jobs in exchange for small amounts of cash.

We identified opportunities to get paid for work that other people did not wish to do.

We realized that some people would be willing to pay someone else for doing those, and other undesirable jobs.

This is the foundation of a capitalist system. I earned my first few cents for work I had done well when I was about 6 years old.

We learned about reward in exchange for work early.

Work hard and enjoy the rewards! Work even harder - or do more things for people who are willing to pay one for that work - and earn even greater rewards.

Good quality production or output equals good rewards.

We fished for our plates, not for fun. Although mostly, it was also fun. We would never catch and release unless we caught something inedible.

We never wasted food.

*****

At school, a classmate would sometimes eat half of his or her lunch sandwich and dump the remainder in the trash can. I would retrieve it and enjoy eating the discarded, and often genuinely nice, homemade sandwich.

Our schools did not have cafeterias. There was no such thing as reduced- or free lunch services as part of a greater social net provided by public service entities.

Children would sometimes spot me picking up and eating their discarded lunch. Some started bringing extra lunch sandwiches to school, for me.

I am sure my brothers learned the same supply, demand, and resourcefulness management strategies at that time, because they were older and smarter. But I was basically being introduced to a study of supply and demand economics... plus philanthropy!

One day, I dreamed, I would be able to supply food and sandwiches, to hungry, homeless people.

*****

Going to school was an escape from *home*. But we also went to school to learn whatever the government had decreed important for us to learn, like children today.

Of course, we were not yet able to spell, let alone discern the meaning of *propaganda*.

My mother had renamed the local newspaper. It was officially called The Daily Dispatch. That is what the header said anyway.

We had some ideas as to why she called the newspaper *The Daily Disgrace*. But we also did not really care. We thought it was just her sense of humor, and we were young.

But really, her renaming of the local newspaper probably played a part in my future distrust of the *mainstream media*, as we know it today.

Childhood indoctrination!

And ironically, *The Daily Disgrace* is the only part of my early childhood education I can vividly recall, from a time when I was about 8 or 9 years of age.

*****

We played after school, unsupervised, and got up to all kinds of mischief.

Some of the mischief was minor, like jumping someone's fence to pick fruit from their backyard orchard. Everyone who owned a house seemed to have fruit trees in their back yard.

Free food!

Sometimes a homeowner would chase us away. At other times, they would step out of the house with a bag or cardboard box and ask us to pick and collect more fruit, to take home. This was mutually beneficial. If left unpicked, fresh fruit would fall to the ground when ripe, start to rot, and then attract bugs and other pests.

*****

Every few months, my mother - late with the previous month's rent and about to be evicted - would tell us that she had found *a new hotel* for us to move to.

This one would be better than the previous one.

That was her sales pitch.

Moving was easy.

We simply gathered our clothes and personal belongings and left the hotel carrying everything by hand. We would walk to the next hotel, typically only a few blocks.

Then, when we arrived at our new residence, we would simply push our respective bags or suitcases under our beds, and the relocation adventure would be complete.

I cannot remember how many times we moved from one hotel or annex to another, but it was at least every few months until I was almost ten years old.

*****

During the time we were living in East London, my oldest brother Gerald had gotten married.

He and his new wife were living together in a small apartment near Cape Town. Not too far from where I had been born about a decade earlier.

Aunt Ruby was Gerald's new mother-in-law.

Around early 1972, Ruby and her husband Jimmy were involved in a horrific motor vehicle collision.

Jimmy died in that accident. As a result, Ruby, and her only son - about the same age as my brother Sean at the time - were living in a comfortable 3-bedroomed house.

Just the two of them, without Uncle Jimmy.

Ruby very kindly offered to have us live with her for a while.

We were homeless and needed help. She perhaps needed some

friendship, love, and companionship.

Today, it might be hard to believe that travel and accommodation arrangements were made by writing and mailing letters or postcards, occasionally making a telephone call, or sending a telegram. Long distance telephone calls and sending telegrams were extraordinarily expensive, especially for people with limited means.

*****

Now, once again, we would relocate to another city.

By train, a two-day, one night journey.

For me, back to my place of birth.

I was about to celebrate my tenth birthday. A birthday present was often a piece of candy, or perhaps one day without any physical punishment.

But, as a family, we were now scattered all over the country.

I mentioned Gerald's whereabouts near Cape Town.

Meanwhile, my sister Maggie had also moved away. She moved north when we relocated south. Pretoria - her new hometown - and Cape Town, are two of South Africa's largest cities, the farthest apart from one another.

My older brother Abe was about to enter his last year at high school right after our planned relocation to Cape Town.

An exceedingly kind family offered to accommodate him, allowing him to finish his high school education in East London without any disruption to his senior year.

So, now there were three of us traveling to Ruby's house.

Goodwood, where her house was located, is a blue-collar, working-class suburb of Cape Town.

The house had three bedrooms: one for Ruby, one for my mother, and one that was shared by Ruby's son and my brother Sean.

My room was the converted, enclosed patio at the back of the house.

It would be challenging to easily describe this incredible upgrade in our living standards.

My mother had her own room for the first time in her life. She was nearly 46 years of age.

Sean shared a room with Ruby's son... a young man of similar age.

My *bedroom* was larger than our previously shared hotel room.

Or at least, that is how it seemed.

It was quite luxuriously appointed. By our standards for sure.

We only lived with Ruby for one year before we would move again. The next move, to Pretoria, would be my mother's final relocation.

*****

We were scheduled to arrive in Pretoria - one of three capital cities in South Africa - by train from Cape Town, towards the end of 1973.

Maggie had helped to convince our mother to relocate to Pretoria. The city was flourishing in the mid-seventies.

Business was booming. Many people had reasonably well-paying government jobs, with great benefits. The city also has several universities, offering a great mix of older and younger people, a vibrant nightlife, many restaurants, world class sporting events and other entertainment.

Pretoria has an amazingly good climate. Summers are hot with occasional showers. Winters are cool to cold, but dry with sunny skies. For most of the year the weather is near perfect.

It took nearly three full days and two nights on a train, to travel from Cape Town to Pretoria.

It might sound romantic and exciting, but it is an incredibly boring and tedious journey. Unless you know how to play and win the royal card game called Solitaire.

There is probably a reason why the game is called Solitaire. To me, it was a fancy word for solitary.

Some people know it by other names, like Patience. This is probably because you need to be patient and hone your skills before you will become proficient at playing Solitaire.

Recently I learned that J.P. Morgan, the world-famous banker, and founder of JPMorgan Chase Bank, played thousands of games of Solitaire in his retirement. When not playing the card game, he spent his time reading. Reading is the least expensive way for anyone to tap into the brilliant minds of greatly successful people. Today, one can easily learn more about Mr. Morgan. The Morgan Library & Museum at Madison Avenue in New York City is magnificent.

Once you figure it out, you will realize that more than 90% of random Solitaire games are winnable. Yes, even when you play online. If you lose too many games or give up too easily when playing Solitaire... you need more patience!

I realized early in my life that I had a skill for calculating and remembering numbers.

Or playing cards. But not any numbers, or random numbers. Logical numbers, sequences, combinations, or perhaps a limited quantity of random numbers, like a complete deck of 52 playing cards.

I liked playing number games.

Any games with combinations of logical moves and elements of chance, like blackjack or backgammon.

I enjoyed estimating and/or calculating my odds of winning a game. Learning when to double or forfeit. Keeping track of victories vs. defeats in number-type games.

I had an aunt whom my siblings and I, as children, referred to as slightly crazy. This rude and incorrect labeling was mostly because of her random, nonstop babbling. She would never stop talking!

We did not know - at the time - that she was a high functioning Autistic, *human computer*.

She was able to remember any numbers, and dates of random events and letters she had received, for example.

I was fascinated with her ability to remember dates. I am not referring to typical dates that people remember, like birthdays, wedding anniversaries, etc. No, she would be able to recall the exact date she received your last letter in the mail three years ago, and so on.

Her math and number memory skills were not readily appreciated or acknowledged. For many reasons. One being that in the 70's women in South Africa mostly entered the workforce only because they had no other choice.

For example, single mothers with children, like my mother. They were generally not able to secure great jobs.

I once observed my aunt adding columns of numbers in a ledger by simply scrolling her pencil - used as a pointer - down a page, adding as she visually followed her pointer.

She was a mathematical genius, but she would never stop talking.

Not knowing any better, as children, we would run away to go and play outside... rather than be subjected to nonstop rambling.

High Functioning Autism.

A unique ability.

*****

I had just celebrated a birthday. I was 11 years old.

We were now three family members still living together in a small, two-bedroomed, rental apartment in Pretoria. My mother was 48 years old. Sean had turned 16 the day before my 11th birthday.

We were content, almost happy.

Life was good.

My mother had a bookkeeping job with a large furniture retail store. Her job was a double win. Despite earning a modest salary, her monthly pay was better than before.

Our apartment rent was affordable.

We were able to purchase furniture for our - initially - empty apartment at pennies to the dollar, and her employer offered his employees very generous repayment terms, and at no interest. The furniture we purchased were mostly repossessed from, or returned by, other clients. Slightly damaged, gently used furniture that looked like it came from very posh homes.

To us anyway.

We had food. We enjoyed simple, but regular meals.

Sometimes we had peanut butter sandwiches for dinner. I still eat this today, and still appreciate it. Occasionally, my mother would buy fancy food, like cheese. We would devour it quickly!

Then, in 1974, my mother became seriously ill. She no longer wanted to go for a walk, a favorite activity.

It was too tiring.

She started losing weight. She would inform me that she needed to spend a few days in the hospital. The doctors would be giving her medicine to make her better.

And then a short while later, she had to go again.

She prayed a lot.

Prayer is comforting for people who have faith, but it is not an effective remedy for people with ailments.

For people blessed with logic and reason, prayer is arguably useless, and ineffective.

This is why *faith healers* never pray for amputees in front of a live audience.

But prayer probably provides comfort in times of distress. My mother was a devout Christian. She fervently believed that her prayers would be answered.

She had always lived a good life.

She never used bad language. She had paid her tithes to her church... even if it were paid from the last little bit of cash she had on hand.

When she had an abundance of anything, she helped others. She was a good person.

Her illness became worse. Adults immediately started whispering when I was within earshot.

I realized that something might be amiss.

But I refused to believe that she would not get better. At the age of 12, one is not expected to be able to even say, let alone understand the scope of a disease known as invasive lobular carcinoma.

Her breast cancer had spread to other parts of her body. It had metastasized, meaning that the cancer cells had broken away from the original tumor, traveled through the blood or lymph system, and formed new tumors in other organs or tissues of the body.

Her condition was beyond *modern medical repair*, let alone prayer!

Then one day, my mother told me she would need to go to hospital for a while longer, to get better.

A couple in her church had offered to accommodate and take care of me for a while. I would go and live with them, maybe for a week or so.

Two nice people. Soft spoken, humble, and kind. A young couple without any children of their own.

I am not sure if they eventually had any children. In a sense, my mere presence in their home for an extended period might have been a most efficacious method of eliminating any desire they may have harbored for future parenthood.

And anyway, a radical new drug - the oral contraceptive pill - offered an end to unwanted pregnancies without negatively impacting sexual pleasure.

The pill was rapidly becoming popular, especially among heathens and sinners, in the 70's.

One week became a month. My mother seemed to spend more time in the hospital, than at home.

We gave up our apartment. We moved most of our furniture to

my sister Maggie and her husband. They had been married for a short while; a young couple at the start of their shared adult life, living in a small, sparsely furnished apartment. They could use whatever we had to discard.

I was in my final year at elementary school. Sean was in his final year of high school.

On December 1, 1975, my mother died.

She was 49.

She would have celebrated her fiftieth birthday a month later, on January 1, 1976.

Her death was five days before I turned 13, and four days before Sean's 18th birthday.

We were now once again, homeless.

However, we were now also orphans.

Our father was still alive, somewhere, but we had not seen or heard anything of him in nearly a decade.

*****

Sean somehow managed to secure acceptance as a trainee police cadet into the police college, located near Pretoria.

Free board and lodging. And uniforms can also be called *free clothing*. Well played Sean!

I was informally adopted by another family from my mother's church.

They took me in, clothed, and fed me. They provided a comfortable, warm bed. The family was nice.

But later, the patriarch was charged and arrested for child molestation.

*****

A few months later, my oldest brother Gerald offered to take me in to live with him and his family, near Cape Town.

Soon, I returned to the city of my birth, relocating from Pretoria, in the middle of my Grade 8 school year.

I moved into their humble home in the winter of 1976.

Cape Town's winters are harsh. Cold, often with driving rain for days on end.

I would ride my bicycle to school.

Sometimes, my school uniform would not properly dry out for weeks on end, despite me wearing an oversized raincoat as an overcoat.

Gerald and his wife had two children.

Two boys. At the time of my arrival, one was a baby, the other four years old. They became my little brothers for the next few years. I was no longer the youngest sibling.

Gerald was 14 years older than me. A physically strong, 27-year-old man.

He became my worst enemy.

This was not only because he would punish me physically.

I felt I was able to handle beatings at the hand of my older brother. Rather, it was his wife who physically abused me. She fervently believed in the Biblical philosophy, *spare the rod... and spoil the child.*

I was exceedingly small for my age, slight of build.

Perhaps this was a result of years of malnutrition? Or perhaps my smaller frame was the visible result of a lack of participation in competitive sporting activities as a child... physical activities that help to build character, in addition to a healthier, stronger physique?

No, my brother became my enemy because he never prevented - nor tried to interfere with - his wife abusing me, his *little* brother.

And at least as far as I were concerned, punishment I received was not commensurate with any of my *crimes*.

The rod was often anything the young wife was able to find when she needed one. Sometimes the rod broke, causing her to search for, and instantly find a replacement.

I would go to school from time to time with red welts on different parts of my body, that would become dark bruises after a couple of days. I was ashamed and desperate, and felt unable to do anything about it. I also lacked an adult mentor or minder to confide in.

Different times!

And ashamed? Yes. Because shame was embedded in our religious upbringing.

Amazing Grace, how sweet the sound.

That saved a wretch like me...

*****

I managed to finish high school while living with Gerald and his family.

During my senior year, I started writing applications for student bursaries.

Americans call these student loans. Bursaries are different from scholarships, because they must either be repaid in full - in the future - or the post-graduate student would be required to work for the bursar for a period matching the total grant funding period e.g., four years.

I planned to secure one or more, as part of an escape plan.

I did not share my plans with anyone. Mainly because I feared having to admit defeat in the event of failure.

The shame of failing!

I did not know any better.

I had not yet learned that trying something and failing would always be far better than not trying anything at all!

Later, as I matured, I learned that failure is the best and most valued tutor.

I applied to only one university for acceptance into a bachelor's degree program, selecting Accountancy as a proposed major.

I completed all the admission application forms myself, and signed them personally, on behalf of my legal guardian.

I did not think to apply to more than one academic institution. No-one had informed me that winning acceptance into a university program was a competitive process.

But the Rand University in Johannesburg accepted and approved my application for admission.

I was a resident of another city and province, some distance away and had no local family - or a fixed address - near the Johannesburg campus.

Therefore, the acceptance letter included a condition: I had to either (a) demonstrate an ability to personally fund the annual fees, or (b) provide proof of a grant award (or similar) that would cover the cost of annual tuition and on-campus accommodation.

Thankfully, the South African Railways awarded me with a bursary. It generously covered the entire annual tuition and on-campus residency fees for the first year of my studies.

It was renewable annually if I achieved a passing grade.

In June 1980, I was delighted to receive notification of this award, matching the university's conditional acceptance of my proposed enrollment as a full-time, on-campus residency student.

I was 17 years of age. Not yet officially and legally entitled to execute contracts... but I had signed them anyway.

*****

For 4 years I had already worked at a local supermarket as a cashier every Friday afternoon after school until 8 PM, when the store closed. On Saturdays I worked from 8 AM to 1 PM.

Those days, most retail shops were closed on Saturday afternoons and Sundays.

I had saved most of the money I earned. I did not pay tithes to any church. I did not contribute to collection plates when these were passed around at church services.

I was trying to recover financially from having been born into poverty.

My mother had often said, "Charity begins at home."

I was never sure exactly what that meant. But assumed that her directive did not support the distribution of any unwarranted or undeserved payments to third parties.

I did not go to parties, movies, or hang out with friends at the local diner.

I conscientiously did my homework, read books, listened to music, played guitar. I would throw a tennis ball into the air and catch it for hours on end.

I had nowhere to spend my hard-earned cash, perhaps somewhat fortuitously.

As a result of my self-imposed isolation and diligence in trying to score high marks for my schoolwork - motivated, at least in part, by a constant fear of being punished - my test scores at school were quite good, an A or B, for most exams.

Furthermore, my school curriculum set me up for reasonable future success. Along with languages, my electives included Science, Mathematics, Business Economics and Accountancy. Of these, I found the latter to be the easiest.

And being lazy of disposition, this last sentence above also explains my desire to enroll for a bachelor's course at university, majoring in accounting.

*****

The university was in South Africa's biggest city, Johannesburg.

Perfect!

I did not have any family in Johannesburg.

I did not want family nearby. I was escaping.

One day - around that same time and about six months before the end of my senior year at high school – Gerald inquired about my future.

Specifically, he wanted to know what my plans were for after finishing high school.

I nonchalantly replied, "I'll be going to university in Johannesburg."

He laughed.

Then, in an endearing, somewhat fatherly and caring manner, he started to explain that with one exception, members of our family had not been able to attend, let alone graduate from university. The intake requirements were extremely strict, the costs prohibitive, and so on.

I listened patiently. Solitaire teaches patience. Inside, I was rolling around on the floor laughing, but I managed to maintain a poker face.

He then asked, "So what are you planning to do?"

I said, more confidently this time, that I would start a bachelor's degree majoring in Accounting in January, 1981. I would attend Rand University in Johannesburg. I had already been awarded a bursary from the *Railways* that covered the cost of my academic studies and on-campus residency in full.

His jaw dropped.

My spirits lifted!

This was my first major victory, after nearly 18-years of miserable defeat and suffering.

He was shocked. Maybe a little impressed, but shocked, nonetheless.

He asked how I would get from Cape Town to Johannesburg... probably wondering if I would require a contribution to my travel costs from his strictly managed, and relatively small, monthly household budget.

I reminded him that my bursary had been awarded to me by *the Railways*, and that it included one free round trip by rail to any domestic destination annually.

As it were, I was planning to only use a single one-way ticket for a dream escape into a new life chapter. One that would be free of misery, parental guidance, and other supervisory interference.

My masterplan unfortunately ignored the fact that students have needs. In addition to clothing, I would also need to purchase textbooks, pay for certain activities and/or memberships on campus, have pocket money available from time to time for discretionary spending, etc.

I might have failed to envisage a complete and detailed strategy for my exit and future success. But I had an escape plan... and vague dreams!

Harold MacMillan, Former Prime Minister of the United Kingdom, famously declared, "It has been said that there is no fool like and old fool, except a young fool. But the young fool has first to grow up to be an old fool to realize what a damn fool he was when he was a young fool.

CHAPTER 2

DOING THE LOCOMOTION

The day after I wrote my final last high school exam, I boarded a train for my solitary journey into the great unknown, *the big smoke*.

Johannesburg was - and the greater surrounding area still is - South Africa's economic capital. It is one of the largest cities in Africa in terms of GDP and population.

I was going to live in the big city.

I was 18 years old, and *finally free*!

The journey by train was once again three days and two nights. I was traveling for free, having cashed in my S.A. Railways annual free travel coupon for employees and contracted students, for the one-way trip.

My travel companions included five men.

During the day the compartment was a cubicle with one long bench either side where three people could sit, facing one another. At night one bench and another one built into the wall above, converted into three beds on each side, or six in total in the compartment.

A tight squeeze, with shared bathroom facilities down the hallway.

That was how second-class rail travel was organized in the 80's.

If you booked a single traveler ticket in a 6-berth compartment, you found yourself introduced to 5 new friends. Sometimes, one might get lucky, and the train would not be full, but that did not happen too often.

My travel companions were hardened journeymen.

Much older.

Working class men traveling at the end of the year, perhaps to visit family for the December holidays.

Sometimes, a traveler would disembark at a city or small town along the way, creating more space and leaving one extra bunk bed in the compartment free and available.

During the day we would talk, play cards, gamble a little with pennies or matches.

They taught me how to do shots of cheap vodka, neat.

They were adults.

I was a small and rather frail boy-child.

When they inquired about my trip, I said I was going to visit family. I did not want to tell them that I was going to go to university the next month.

They were blue-collar laborers, not academics!

Somehow, I imagined that sharing information about my university plans might imply that I thought myself to be better than them, superior in some way. I was not.

And I needed to remain humble and vigilant.

I had all my cash tucked into one sock.

The local currency is called the South African rand. I had about R100… a small fortune!

No-one had told me that the train journey excluded food, but I managed not to spend any money.

Every time the train stopped at a station, one or a few of the guys would disembark to purchase food at the station café. They would return with way too much food for one person.

Humans generally tend to gather, collect, and consume too much stuff, including too much food when hungry.

As it were, almost every time someone purchased supplies, they were unable to finish the food. Then they would offer me - or the others - whatever was left.

They laughed and joked, saying things like, "Give the skinny kid the food."

And I would laugh with them, and then eat whatever they had decided to give me.

The only drink we had was vodka. I am not sure shots of cheap vodka was enjoyable, but I also did not know any better or different.

They drank far more than what they shared with me, which was probably a good thing. I only became a little inebriated. My travel companions were smashed most of the time and slept for extended periods, while I played solitaire.

Occasionally I would drink brackish water from the train's water fountain. That was worse than the cheap vodka.

I managed to retain my entire stash of cash for the duration of the journey. Hidden safely inside one sock. It was not even at risk at any time during the journey, because I did not change my socks, not even once.

*****

I arrived in Johannesburg 3 days later.

Maggie drove to meet me at the station.

She had insisted.

Maggie had married her boyfriend a few years prior.

They lived in a small mining town located a couple of hours east of Johannesburg. Her husband was a newly qualified young dentist, starting out in private practice.

Those days, one only traveled to the big city for a special event or occasion. This time, my arrival for an extended visit after a 5-year absence was the occasion.

She drove us to their house.

They were nice to me. Maggie and her husband. My brother-in-law is one of the kindest people I have ever met.

We had only spent limited time together when I was a child, and before they were married.

We did not have opportunities to connect at a personal level during our brief interactions during those earlier years. The age-gap between us was too great a chasm. This is especially true when one person might be a child aged 12 and the other, a young man aged about 24.

I stayed with them for more than a month. They were great hosts and welcoming, and I had nowhere else to go anyway.

At the time, the university residences only allowed on-campus resident students to arrive on or after mid-January for the start of the new academic school year.

*****

I had previously had extraordinarily little life coaching, arguably perhaps, none.

For sure, no-one had ever taken the time to explain that *with great freedom comes great responsibility*!

Suddenly, as if in a flash, I was introduced to on-campus college life. It was the start of the 80's. Rock music, flower-power and free love of the 60's …had been replaced with disco pop, casual sex, *big hair*, and recreational drugs.

Everyone was friendly.

Many students were just there to have fun, not learn.

Suddenly, my previous *solitary confinement* and lack of social skills and interaction left me bewildered. All the things I had been exposed to, or forced into previously: religion, school uniforms, supervision, punishment, etc. were now all, suddenly, strikingly absent.

No-one went to church. We wore whatever clothes we felt like wearing. Sometimes the young female students were scantily clad, even quite provocatively. If one had elected not to attend classes, there seemed to be no consequences.

I needed to find work. Earn money. My stash of cash had only lasted a few weeks.

Some students, especially the juniors and seniors, had part-time jobs.

Many students did not need to work because their parents gave them allowances that covered their basic needs.

But I needed money!

I had some skills and work experience from before, and that made me feel bulletproof. I was not afraid to do any type of work that would earn me some money. If it were legal.

I discovered that one of the best paying, but worst jobs - according to those who knew - was selling encyclopedias.

Students thought it was awful because it required cold-calling and selling door-to-door. Two of the most off-putting requirements of any entry-level sales job, for most people.

But very often the worst jobs were also the best paying jobs, out of necessity. When it is tough for corporations to attract, recruit and retain employees, they are often forced to pay higher wages.

As it were, I became a door-to-door encyclopedia salesman.

Now I was suddenly introduced to an environment where people would shout at me, threaten me for trespassing onto their properties, refuse to answer the door even though I could easily tell that they were home, and more.

But every so often I managed to find a customer and close a sale.

The commission earned for a closed deal was particularly good at around R50 (fifty rand) per set of books sold.

Remember, earlier I shared that my journey into adulthood had begun with R100 tucked into my one sock? Now, I was earning that amount - previously my life's savings - every few days.

It was also possible to earn bonuses for selling add-ons, like bookcases, or a subscription for annual reference book updates. If we sold three sets of books in one week, we would earn an extra R20.

I was quickly learning to understand performance-based earnings. Working for commission on executed sales contracts only meant that the more I sold, the more I earned.

Earnings commensurate with effort was, and remains, a wonderful motivational tool for growth-minded entrepreneurs and businesspeople in general.

Soon, I was earning about R500 per month, working only a few hours, a couple of days per week. Sometimes, I would earn half of that amount over one weekend.

The sales team went out selling when our team leader - who had a car - drove us out into some swanky area. A leafy, upscale suburb where rich people lived.

We looked for homes that offered visible signs of children in the household. Toys or playscapes in the backyard.

Telltale signs of people who might be willing and able to afford a large amount of money for a set of home encyclopedias. Poorer people had to send their kids to the library for reference lookups.

Also, a compendium of books, neatly displayed, looked impressive on a shelf!

Parents were willing to purchase our products because they wanted to ensure that their kids were offered the best education available, as parents often do.

We would introduce ourselves with some elevated level of standing when homeowners opened and greeted us at their front door.

I would say something like, "Good afternoon. I am Rudi Bester from South African Cultural Investments (there was no such corporation). We are doing a short survey in your neighborhood about educational tools for children of school age. May I come in and ask you a few questions?"

We were smartly dressed. Guys wore suits, dress shirts and neckties. Young ladies wore pretty dresses with matching shoes and sensible heels.

We were trained to look the part. To be professional. Serious. Our offerings were meant to ensure a brighter future for their highly educated, and better-informed children!

It was also my introduction into sales.

A foundation for a future career as a sales professional.

I learned to present a product. And how to manage and over-come rejection, sales objections, and how to deal with some-times rather difficult people.

I am referring to an organic sales process. One where one must learn the product, identify prospects who might become poten-tial clients, navigate through a scalable and repeatable process, and execute deals.

Net, new, organic sales is quite different from *upsell or add-on* sales done by account managers or customer relations-type em-ployees. These often start with the client initiating the sales op-portunity. True sales professionals would patronizingly refer to someone selling products to existing clients as *order-takers*.

This is also true when one is required to deploy a client retention strategy of sorts, when an existing client relationship is at risk. It is less expensive to retain a client, than to find a new client!

When faced with a client relationship at risk, career account and/or relationship managers might be well advised to step aside and delegate *the save* to a salesperson.

Borrowing from a sports analogy… a true sales professional is like a designated hitter in baseball. The person entrusted with hitting a home run when the bases are loaded, or when one run would secure a victory.

I now considered myself more of a businessman than a student.

My monthly earnings from selling sets of encyclopedias would potentially easily eclipse the future earnings of a professionally licensed and certified accountant… if I were to do it as a full-time gig.

And anyway, who would want to sit in an office all day, crunching numbers, when a kid straight out of high school could out-earn them... while working whenever and only when they felt like working?

*****

I had been offered an extraordinary opportunity to attend university and to achieve an educational qualification way beyond what might have been possible for someone of my humble and disadvantaged background.

A chance at a future professional career in a white-collar field that just a few years prior would have been unimaginable. But I was not entirely convinced that being an accountant would be my preferred, future career path.

My heart was not in the space, and therefore my mind kept wandering.

The idea of working for the Railways as a junior bookkeeper for four years post-graduation also did not seem overly enticing.

I had spent a few weeks working for my bursar during a university vacation. It was a requirement that all students who received funding support were required to intern for a few weeks, every year.

It was horrible!

I became increasingly convinced that a lifetime profession as *a bean counter* would not be well suited to my disposition.

*****

I was a terrible student, even though I managed to scrape by passing my first-year major and a few other subjects. I absolutely detested Statistics!

The concept of being required to analyze and interpret sets of data that did not provide an absolute conclusion or prove anything, did not sit well.

Statistics 101 was a required credit. That made it even more annoying.

Here is a recent example of how statistics is used to influence and encourage *group think*:

The mainstream media would tout their latest polling results related to the upcoming (2016) U.S. election. The result of their poll would inform voters that "The chances of Hillary Clinton winning the election was 85%".

In this instance above, they had basically announced a forgone conclusion to a major upcoming event. News likely shared to help influence the outcome of the election and/or to support of a preferred political narrative.

Of course, they did not provide more details.

And they neglected to mention that - using their own results - that there would be a 15% chance that Ms. Clinton might lose the election.

However, in terms of statistical probability, this last statement is as meaningless as the aforesaid. Especially when viewed in isolation as a media *sound bite*; lacking context to the audience that had been polled, the time of day, period and/or duration of the poll, their polling methodology employed, the current news cycle that may have impacted results, and more.

Another questionable statistic is the mortality rate of the recent coronavirus pandemic.

The number is incorrect unless we had tested 100% of the deceased and determined without any doubt, via an autopsy, that their deaths were not caused because of another preexisting condition or comorbidity.

Also, deaths should have been recorded as dying *from* rather than *with* COVID-19 as the primary cause of death for the statistic to have any foundational, scientific validity.

*****

The Accounting 101 curriculum at university included the entire three years of high school accounting - that I had been so successful at - during the first three months of my first year at university.

This meant that any advantage I might have had over high school graduates who had not elected Accounting as a school subject, was quashed within a few weeks!

I was learning about competitive advantage.

I needed to find an edge, a way to outperform my peers without having to do more work than them.

I referred to my competitive advantages as *Power Positions*.

I had none.

My fellow students were at least as smart as I had considered myself to be.

Furthermore, their backgrounds and upbringings were superior. They had families, support structures, their basic needs met. These were features and benefits I had never even thought of or considered as being beneficial to one's success and/or progress in life, or career, because one cannot know what one does not know.

I needed to plan a warpath for victory, or otherwise an escape, once more.

But this time, my dilemma offered an added twist:

Freedom from the academic institution would be easy - after all, I could just up, and leave - but I now had this added responsibility of refunding my bursar's loan, with interest.

And I would owe significantly more money than I had, or could possibly earn, within a reasonable amount of time, by selling encyclopedias door to door.

That is the thing about debt. When required to service debt obligations, a debtor requires earnings that exceed whatever income he or she might require for their usual, day-to-day living expenses.

Smart people call *debt* by another word... *leverage*.

I had to figure this out, quickly.

*****

At the start of my second year at university, I declined funding from my bursar.

For as long as I was a full-time student, I would not be required to service the existing debt obligation, although the amount owing would attract interest.

Without servicing the capital balance outstanding I would end up owing more and more. I was learning the mechanisms and compounding costs of consumer debt.

An ever-increasing amount of outstanding debt was unacceptable.

I needed a plan.

I remained an enrolled student. But by now I was only attending classes once or twice a week.

A friend at university helped me - by way of a personal introduction - to secure a job as a proofreader at a local newspaper. This job would provide a regular income stream, rather than unpredictable, occasionally earned sales commissions.

I started working night shifts for The Citizen. A government-funded, propaganda tabloid that was specifically created to help prop up South Africa's minority government during the apartheid years.

I was blissfully unaware of the above, learning later that some people had dismissed this as a conspiracy theory.

When one is young, ignorant, and gullible there appears to be no logical reason to distrust elected political *leaders* or people in positions of authority... like preachers, or teachers.

When the truth finally surfaced, as it always does, the facts proving government control of my ex-employer were obvious, and overwhelming.

Proofreaders were human versions of what people might think of today as automated word processing, or artificial intelligence software that offers spelling and grammar corrections as is typing.

In our newspaper editing room we - all young male students - worked in pairs.

One person would read newspaper articles that had been typed by journalists, aloud. He was the *proofreader*.

The other would hold a copy. The *copyholder* would follow along, listen, and call a pause to make spelling and grammar corrections on one of the typed sheets that we were working with.

Then, we would send the edited article back to the presses for setting and printing.

This had to be completed before 3 AM for the morning edition to hit the streets on time.

Print setters would express frustration and anger if we had made only minor corrections - like adding a comma or splitting one long sentence into two or more short sentences - because this nuisance arguably required more work than its worth.

After 3 AM we went home.

The next evening, we would return at 9 PM for the following night's shift.

It was a terrible job, but if I worked 6 days a week, I could easily pay back the interest and even some of the capital.

I was learning to service a financial debt obligation and its interest expense. Money earned today, was first applied to the repayment of debt incurred in the past.

It seemed as if my earnings were diluted due to previous errors in judgment.

I had purchased something I was unable to afford and/or used debt to finance an aspiration.

This is vastly different to a company - or a person - using debt to finance business expansion, machinery, new products or services, an entry into a new market, etc.

Debt can be good when used correctly.

If only they taught us that at school!

*****

One day, I was walking home after my night shift.

It must have been between 3-4 AM. I walked past a Holiday Inn hotel. The lobby was lit, and the hotel seemed glitzy and glamorous inside.

This hotel was not like the hotels we had lived in when I was a child.

The President's Holiday Inn in Johannesburg, at the time, was an upmarket skyscraper, twenty stories high.

But the hotel had nineteen floors, because the 13th floor was missing.

I walked into the reception area. A friendly young lady greeted and welcomed me, like a guest.

With a touch of bravado, I asked her if the hotel was hiring any staff.

She smiled. I was not used to random, unknown people being friendly.

She said that the Food & Beverage (F&B) Manager was in his office, working the night shift.

Then she added that he would probably hire me on the spot because the hotel was short-staffed in their banqueting and room service divisions, and desperate to hire.

I was immediately back into my door-to-door salesman mode.

"The F&B Manager was desperate to hire?", I thought to myself.

My imagined *asking price* automatically went higher.

I made my way to his office, as directed. Like most people who work in hospitality, he looked up when I approached and cheerfully greeted me, flashing a friendly smile.

Hotels only seem to hire people who can smile spontaneously and always appear to be happy.

He asked how he might be able to assist.

I said something along the lines of, "a good friend had told me that the hotel needed some staff to help with banqueting management."

If one is to take a chance, you might as well promote yourself at least one position higher than the obvious staffing requirement.

He smiled. If he saw right through my fake bravado, he did not allow me to notice.

He asked me whether I would be able to work under pressure, whether I would be comfortable speaking to guests over the telephone and listen attentively to their requests, organize, and arrange food orders in terms of priority and timing, and about my availability to work shifts.

The impromptu interview went well. We were both desperate, but neither wanted to be obvious.

He said that if I were able to start immediately, he could offer me a job as Room Service Manager at a monthly salary of R400.

Room Service *Manager* was a lofty title for the person a guest would speak to when calling room service to order a meal or drinks for delivery to their hotel room.

This example of immediacy or urgency was how recruiting was generally managed in many different industry verticals - e.g., manufacturing, hospitality, retail and many more - one generation ago.

People walked into corporate offices, manufacturing plants or retail stores, for example, found a human to speak to and simply said, "I'm looking for a job."

Very few candidates had formal, typed resumes.

Few people owned typewriters, and personal computers had not yet been invented. Some people took the time and trouble to prepare a neat, handwritten CV for a particular job opening but most people did not.

Face-to-face contact, honest discussion (assumed) and firm handshakes sealed business deals, rather than e.g., paper, or electronic versions of personal marketing collateral, outlining one's experience and skills.

The offer he made created a small window of opportunity for me to negotiate. But I had no hospitality-related *Power Positions*. This conversation was entirely centered around his urgent need and my availability.

I meekly countered with a bluff, saying that my friend had told me the starting salaries were R500 per month, not R400.

He politely said that *my friend* had been wrong about that. But, an hour later, he hired me into a new job with a starting salary of R450 per month.

This proposed based salary was basically the same as my monthly earnings at Citizen newspaper. But hospitality offers more, diversified opportunities to earn money, as I will explain below.

My first overnight shift started that very same evening, about 14 hours after my initial interview.

Just time for a nap in between. No celebration. Just a young, single guy busy hustling; selling time and labor in exchange for cash compensation.

I did not have to give notice to quit my job at the Citizen.

People in the proofreading department came and went.

The proofreaders and copyholders were all students.

If one or two departed it did not matter because there were always a few applicants waiting in line. The same as it was on the day when I just arrived and then started working, that very same day.

I worked in the room service department for about a month. That is how long it took me to meet and get friendly with the hotel's bartenders.

They earned tax-free, cash gratuities on top of their monthly salary, which was like mine.

I became a bartender. Therefore, soon after my arrival, I had effectively managed to double my base wage without doubling my hours.

As a result of my rapid transfer from room service to bartending, the banqueting section was once again short-staffed and the F&B Manager again desperate to hire… back to interviewing walk-in candidates, just like before.

*****

CHAPTER 3

READY, FIRE... AIM

One day, while I was working at the Holiday Inn, Maggie tracked me down.

She had called the hotel and managed to connect because I was on duty, working at one of the bars.

She had news.

My father died.

He had been living in a small room in their backyard for a few years. I had seen him once or twice since the day he had left us to fend for ourselves.

I had no relationship with him.

It was 1982.

I was nearly 20 years old.

*****

That same year the South African Army wrote to notify me that

I had to report for military service.

The Defense Force conscription model at the time was affectionately called national service. It had become a mandatory, two-year service period.

You may recall my earlier mention of my brother Gerald's national 9-month service obligation. He had been *called up* for national service about a decade prior.

The government had changed the rules.

This service requirement exclusively for young white men was a mandate from South Africa's minority government, during the apartheid years.

Contrary to popular belief, discrimination is prevalent and pervasive everywhere and affects many people adversely - albeit differently - based on religion, race and/or gender, respectively.

In my instance, my choice was either two years of mandatory national service, or six years imprisonment for refusing to do military service.

Both options are similar, save for the fact that one offers release after two years, the other... six.

Neither offered a chance of early release or parole for good behavior.

A relatively easy choice!

*****

At the age of nineteen, I made my first ever call to a lawyer, asking for an appointment. She - the lawyer - was a junior counsel working for the South African Railways.

The Railways held a note for my student debt.

I wanted to know how they would manage the outstanding debt and related payment commitments if I were to report to the army for two years of conscripted national service.

She explained that they would not be able to take any legal action against me for non-payment of the student loan while I was doing national service.

But she also reminded me that *The Railways* would add interest to the outstanding debt, and that there would be no interest or debt forgiveness.

The interest would obviously cause the total balance of debt outstanding to start compounding and grow significantly higher if I did not make any payments for two years.

I could do the math myself.

I was now acquiring new insight into the principle of compounded capital growth, while learning about the real cost of debt. One could obviously apply this same knowledge to investment growth and wealth creation, but that would only dawn upon me much later in life.

It made me realize why credit card companies were so keen to get one of their cards in your wallet. Of course, once they had succeeded, they would aggressively entice you to use that credit card, to buy things you cannot afford.

At the time, I still owed more than R2,000.

My initial debt burden had been about R3,500. If I made no payments for two years, the outstanding balance would be back at around R3,000 or more by the time I had completed national service.

I had previously imagined that my next payment would have reduced the total amount outstanding to about half of the balance outstanding.

And now this!

Even though the army would accommodate, clothe, and feed me... a recruit doing basic training - at the time - only earned a monthly stipend of about R40.

*****

My father's death created a minor, unexpected windfall.

He had left a few assets for distribution to his heirs.

His total estate was only worth a few thousand Rand. The two most valuable single items, respectively, were a used compact Datsun car and a Kawasaki motorcycle. Both were in relatively good condition and mechanically sound.

My brother Abe was a student. He needed a car. I was about to start national service. I did not own a vehicle. I had been hitch-hiking and using public transport to get around.

Our three other siblings were already somewhat settled in their lives and careers. None of them expressed any interest in a used Datsun or a Kawasaki motorcycle.

Between the five inheritors, we distributed the estate's meager assets amicably and easily.

Abe inherited the car.

I inherited the motorcycle.

*****

In the meantime, I had signed my *call-up* papers for military service.

Basic training would start in January 1983.

I worked at the Holiday Inn for a few more months, and then quit to join the army.

Soon I reported for military service, as instructed, at the S.A. Army's Personnel Services unit. My base unit was in a huge military compound located just outside of the western city limits of Pretoria.

Three months of basic training awaited new recruits upon arrival.

They informed me that after completing my basic training, I could either sign up for a leadership program, or I would automatically be assigned to work in the payroll office.

The latter... because of my recent accounting studies at university. The army needed people who could probably count and do basic math, to help with monthly payroll administration.

This last option would be horrible because Accounting was the job I had been attempting to escape from. But I had a few months before I would be required to decide.

I was one of a couple of thousand new recruits.

Soldier number *78448966*.

Other military unit commanders, or their proxies, visited our base camp from time to time, looking to recruit some of our new, young soldiers to join their units.

It was a sales gig for those unit commanders.

They were trying to recruit soldiers who already had a unique skill or expertise (e.g., a mechanic); people who wanted to experience a certain military activity (e.g., drive a tank); soldiers who perhaps had a special interest in a particular area (e.g., radio or satellite communication); or people who simply wanted to escape an assignment, like payroll administration.

After all, people are different!

Some are suited to jumping out of a perfectly functioning air-craft with a parachute... and other people, less so.

To each, his own!

One such recruiting unit that came calling was S.A. CAT - the South African Army's Catering Division.

It was affectionately named CAT School.

A new friend who was doing basic training with me suggested that working as a cook was better than most other army jobs. His reasoning was sound. At the very least, one would never go hungry. And then, he questioned whether any service men or women would dare to be nasty with the person who had pre-pared his or her food.

Smart!

I signed up to join CAT after completion of my basic training.

Basic training includes learning to stay busy and to keep mov-ing. A moving target is hard to hit. Not just militarily, but even philosophically.

After a few months, I transferred.

A few weeks after arriving at my new base camp, I suffered an unfortunate injury.

While jumping off a slow-moving vehicle, I lost my balance and landed badly, ending up with a fractured bone in my pelvis called an ischial fracture. Fractures of the ischium and pubis are quite common in young athletes, usually a result of falls or similar accidents.

In general, the army does not take kindly to people who are not healthy, fit, and mobile. It is also tough to allocate meaningful work to people who are immobile, and the army generally does not appreciate dependency.

I ended up doing administrative tasks in my base unit's field hospital. Filling in forms for soldiers who reported sick, mopping the floors, painting the walls, sterilizing equipment, and doing other exciting daily tasks.

We played backgammon when no-one was watching.

Literally... thousands and thousands of backgammon games. After a while one becomes so proficient and expert that you can move your pips about the board without much thought. Pro moves are standard, while rolling the dice provides the element of risk, reward, and luck.

Today, I would likely beat an average, casual backgammon player eight or nine times out of ten. The one or two losses would mainly be attributed to unlucky rolls of the dice.

As a result, I mostly play backgammon on a computer at expert level.

I do not like to make people feel like losers.

I still play backgammon when I am not playing Solitaire. Both are perfect accompaniments for boring conference calls.

And a computer never declines a challenge.

*****

As mentioned, the motorbike I inherited turned out to be an unexpected financial windfall.

I scouted for a permanent force member - i.e., someone who works for the army full-time - who might be interested in buying my motorcycle.

My asking price was R2,500. After a few weeks I managed to find a buyer and sold it for R2,200.

On the Friday afternoon of my first weekend pass from CAT, I walked into the S.A. Railways lawyers' offices unannounced. I delivered a cash payment to settle my debt in full, along with interest that had accrued since the last payment I had made a few months earlier.

Free and clear of debt!

But another 18 months of military service awaited.

My injury had allowed me the luxury of remaining in the field hospital. My fracture had almost healed. Most of the officers, drill sergeants, and ranking staff had seen me working at the field hospital every day.

They had gotten familiar with me. I was attending to their direct reports on a regular basis, their family members when they fell ill from time to time, and so on.

And when I was not busy playing backgammon, I served my patients professionally and treated everyone with respect.

It is possible that my previous work experience in hospitality had helped to hone my service-related approach to my work, and my generally warm and welcoming disposition when having to deal with clients.

I was polite, respectful, and helpful.

Most of the time.

I only added a shot of Dettol to a visiting senior officer's coffee occasionally. When they inquired about a strange *after-taste* to their coffee, my mates and I would apologize and say that the mug had probably been in the sterilizer, or something similar. We could always make another cup of coffee.

For some unknown reason they generally declined any immediate offer of a replacement coffee but returned on another day anyway. The hospital was a great place to take a short break and rest for a while. It was clean, welcoming, and offered shelter from the hot African sun.

But I also spent my time learning. First aid, resuscitation, reading prescriptions, emergency medical care, and more.

Within a few weeks the medical doctor - in his capacity as Commanding Officer, Medical Services - requested my formal transfer to the hospital as a full-time medical orderly. He wanted to retain my services and ensure that I would not be sent back to CAT School for training as a cook, after he had spent much of his time training me.

He submitted a request to CAT Command. The reassignment request was approved. My service record was transferred from S.A. CAT to S.A. Medical Services (SAMS), completing the requested reassignment.

In real terms, this meant a new beret and insignia for my uniform, but no change to my everyday work, or place of work.

SAMS started training me as an Operational (or Ops) Medic. This is also known as Emergency Medical Services (EMS) training in several other countries.

It was a win-win.

I had already had some training and experience working as a medic. I was doing good work in between backgammon games.

I was immediately appointed as a non-commissioned officer at the hospital, earning the rank of Lance Corporal.

The military deemed it important for Ops Medics to have a higher rank than a private soldier, i.e., one without any rank. This helps to avoid having Ops Medics challenged when issuing emergency, medical evacuations, or other instructions to field soldiers, and improves expectations that orders would be obeyed.

Six months later, I was promoted to Corporal Bester.

My army pay had shot up commensurate with my respective promotions, from about R40 per month during basic training to almost R120 per month as a Corporal.

My expenses were effectively zero.

My accommodation, food and clothing needs were met by the Army.

I did not smoke or drink beer, which minimized any discretionary spending. At CAT there was always free food and juice available, and I did not have a sweet tooth. I hardly ever purchased snack foods.

I was now learning the foundation and basics of real-life profit and loss (P&L) management.

Money in, money out.

Learning to understand a balance sheet would follow later.

At university, our prescribed textbooks contained financial theory. This was real.

Cash flow. Two of the four most important words for aspiring entrepreneurs to learn in money management.

Another two words - Assets and Liabilities - are foundational for investors who study corporate fundamentals for investment purposes... comprising the two most important sections of a balance sheet.

*****

During my military service period, I met Debbie, my future wife.

On a weekend pass, I hitchhiked to visit Maggie and her husband at their home in a small town, Springs, located a couple of hours away from my army base camp.

That Friday evening, I went to a coffee bar at the invitation of a friend.

There I saw a beautiful young lady, busily chatting with some friends. She was the center of their attraction.

She was wearing a short skirt. She had the most gorgeous, athletic legs I had ever seen. Toned and tanned, with calf muscles like a ballerina.

I glanced in her direction every few minutes, while trying to pretend that I was paying attention to my buddies who were busy telling bad jokes and chatting.

One of my friends prompted me to sing a couple of songs.

I had not performed for a while but had been singing in church since the age of around 6. I was quite comfortable playing guitar and singing in front of a live audience.

Someone handed me a guitar. I sang a Kris Kristofferson song that was popular at the time.

Now, Debbie noticed me.

I was unaware that she was about to compete in a singing competition and that she needed guitar accompaniment for one talent section.

A stroke of good fortune!

A mutual friend introduced us.

I was 20.

Debbie was 15, that day we first met.

*****

During the second year of my military service, I was spending increasingly more time in the field hospital's pharmacy.

The doctor was charged with seeing patients, writing prescriptions, and dispensing medicines.

Those were the rules.

As is custom, rules are meant to be broken. I had become the resident *pharmacist*. I had been dispensing prescription drugs every day for more than a year. If I could not read a prescription, I would simply ask the doctor - who was right next door - to clarify or decipher his bad writing, as is international custom in the general relationship between doctors and chemists.

Furthermore, if I thought that the doctor might have made an error, I informed and/or questioned him. Any drug dispenser should be confident in their knowledge of typical strengths, dosage, and/or quantities of commonly prescribed drugs.

Sometimes I would be correct.

Many times, I was wrong.

But I was learning on the fly.

I also learned that most of the drugs that we were dispensing were generic drugs manufactured by a local company, called Lennon Limited.

I paid special attention to all Lennon drugs, because I was starting to plan my future.

About 3 months before I finished my national service, I wrote a letter to Lennon Limited. Those days, email did not exist, and I did not have ready access to a telephone.

So, I penned a request for employment.

I explained that I was intimately familiar with their generic medicines, briefly described my training as an Ops Medic and my dispensing role in the pharmacy. I named some of their popular drugs and explained the purpose and efficacy of those medications, based on my limited experience.

I ended my letter with bold statements which you might by now, recognize as my Power Positions.

My sales pitch included a unique value proposition, much like this:

1. "It would be easier to train me than any other new hire. Bridging gaps in my existing knowledge would be far easier than training someone else from scratch.
2. If Lennon Limited aspires to generating increased sales revenue, Lennon should hire a salesperson who was able to successfully sell encyclopedias door-to-door. Such raw sales skills are easily transferred to selling quality pharmaceutical products.
3. I have spent nearly two years in the military. I am fit, disciplined, energetic, trustworthy, and hardworking."

I sealed the envelope, addressed it to the Sales Manager, dropped it in the mail, and waited. A few weeks later, I received a reply via mail.

The Sales Manager for the Pharmaceutical Division wanted to know when I would be available to come for an interview.

His business card provided his office number. I arranged a call during working hours and we spoke on the phone. We arranged a day and time to meet. I then asked the doctor for some time off to go for a job interview.

The Sales Manager, Jon Budge, hired me as a Sales Representative for Lennon Limited. Start date, early January 1985.

My two years of military service ended late December 1984. About ten days later, I started at my first professional job.

Starting salary: R1,200 plus commission on sales, plus a company car.

I was a pharmaceutical sales representative.

*****

About two and a half years after we had first met, Debbie agreed to marry me. She was about to turn 18, so we needed her parent's notarized signature to secure a marriage license.

As part of our preparations for future married life, I had rented a small, one-bedroomed apartment and furnished it with a combination of good, used furniture and a few new items.

We were two young people in love. We had meager earthly possessions. We were both from broken homes, but we had found one another, as if by design.

*****

I worked for Lennon Limited for only one year and a few months. During that time, I successfully managed to secure a new job with a Johnson & Johnson subsidiary, Janssen-Cilag.

Although my salary would be about the same as my monthly gross income at Lennon, the prestige of carrying a J&J business card, and dressing in a suit and tie every day, instantly elevated me to the upper echelons of an imagined hierarchy of professional pharmaceutical sales representatives.

There were few companies on the planet that were more prestigious to work for. J&J in the eighties was a revered employer, much like e.g., Apple Inc. is today.

To be fair, J&J still holds similar status in the pharmaceutical industry. It is arguably one of the best-managed pharmaceutical corporations on the planet.

I dedicated myself to achieving success.

I had a co-dependent life partner.

Success was not an aspiration or option.

It was required and expected!

*****

CHAPTER 4

HE AIN'T HEAVY, HE'S MY BROTHER

My brother became my worst enemy.

Those were my words in an earlier chapter, describing my strained and unfriendly relationship with my oldest brother, Gerald.

I had not seen him or his wife in nearly five years.

During that time, Gerald had left his job. When I left his house, he had been working for Kodak in Cape Town.

In the meantime, they had relocated to a city near Johannesburg.

Geographically, we were close. Otherwise, not really. In fact, we had hardly spoken to one another in those five years.

During that 5-year gap, I had attended university full-time for a couple of years, spent two more years in the army, and now I was a hot-shot pharmaceutical sales rep. In my own imagination anyway.

I was still busy growing up.

It is a slow and laborious task… learning to become an adult in the absence of guidance provided by parents, and skilled, successful mentors.

I could not replace my parents, but anyone can work to identify and source great mentors.

Gerald had become a self-employed, small business entrepreneur.

He had identified, and then successfully acquired ownership of a photographic retail store that was in an upmarket shopping mall.

The shop had been part of a once successful chain of franchised retail camera stores. The franchisor had shocked everyone by filing for bankruptcy.

Gerald reached out to me. He wanted to know if Debbie and I would be willing to come and visit them at their home. Join them for a family barbeque. I agreed, albeit with trepidation.

We visited.

Our discussions were cordial and polite. Like a first business meeting perhaps, even though we were family, and even though I had previously lived with them for more than 4 years.

I had matured - at least a little - and they had probably matured a little as well.

Their two young boys were older, one already in his teens. Their financial situation appeared to have improved significantly. They seemed reasonably happy. He told me about the business he had acquired, and I told him about my new job.

We ate, drank wine, and chatted.

Spending time with them was okay.

*****

Meanwhile, at Johnson & Johnson, I was earning performance bonuses. I had been awarded "Rookie of the Year" in 1986.

A few months later, I was promoted and transferred to another city as Regional Manager for the East Coast and Central regions of South Africa.

This promotion was accompanied by a higher income, greater bonuses, a better company car, larger expense account, etc. This was how large corporations compensated their employees in the eighties. It might still be the same today, but I cannot be sure.

I had now been promoted to sales management, much like Jon Budge, who had hired me straight out of the army for my first job at Lennon Limited.

It seemed like a lifetime ago, but only two years had gone by.

Suddenly, my job required P&L responsibility, and I had direct reports.

I was 24 years old, about to turn 25.

*****

Then one day, Gerald called me.

He asked if we could get together. A meetup would not be easy, because I was living and working in Durban on the South African east coast, and he lived near Johannesburg near his retail shop.

The distance between us was about 400 miles, about six hours apart by car, one way.

However, the figurative distance between us in terms of brotherly love might have exceeded the geographical gap significantly.

But people forget, heal, and overcome. This is simply a part of human evolutionary DNA.

During the 80's, commercial air travel was considered a luxury and utilized sparingly as an out-of-pocket expense.

I suggested that the next time I was required to visit Johannesburg for J&J business, we could meet up one evening.

A few months later we managed to meet up at a city hotel on a Saturday afternoon. More like a meeting between two businessmen, and less like a meeting between two brothers.

No lunch, limited small talk, *not hanging out*.

Just a business meeting.

He showed me his business' profit and loss statements.

The statements of financial activities were good. Then he walked me through his balance sheet. His business' financial position was also good. Both were in fact particularly good. It was a very profitable small business!

He only had four full-time employees, including himself. Another four part-time employees - all students - aided over weekends and during vacation periods.

Gerald needed my help. He was looking for operational assistance. The business was growing but he was no longer able to cope with general management responsibilities.

He spent most of his time doing admin. He seemed to like doing administration-type work, and he was very efficient at it. But that meant that he was absent as a floor manager for the retail business. He was not managing the staff, the inventory, pricing, merchandising, etc.

He asked me what my salary was at Johnson & Johnson. I told him that my base salary was R3,000 per month. I earned performance bonuses and drove a fancy, mid-level company car.

He offered me a job and said he would match my current income.

I was a little confused. This was unexpected.

My brother, who had been my enemy, was offering me a job. This was happening more than 6 years after I had meticulously planned my escape from a house of horrors.

His house!

But we had spent some time apart, and seemingly we had both matured a little along the way.

*****

I returned to my home in Durban.

A day later, that Monday after the weekend trip to Johannesburg, I spoke to my J&J manager on the phone.

He knew about Gerald's retail business. I had mentioned it a few times before during casual conversations, and he had also shopped there before.

I told him that Gerald had asked me to join him in his business.

My boss responded, "What took him so long? We were wondering for how long we would be able to retain your services."

Although his response seemed like a genuinely nice compliment, it took me by surprise.

Suddenly, at this stage of my short, but rapidly evolving professional career, I was learning some exceptional people management skills and tips that would be useful in the future.

Years later, I would work to help free people from my employment, if those people were better suited to potentially achieve success elsewhere.

There is a fundamental difference between simply laying people off and working with them to help secure a chance at a better and brighter future, for example, with another employer. I have done both and prefer the latter.

And we all probably know some people managers who say, "It's all about the people", while lacking sincerity.

My manager had hired me, trained me, promoted me, and transferred me to another city. And now he was literally voicing his encouragement for me to consider quitting the job he was paying me to do. He explained that this life event was a learning opportunity. An example of a situation where one must consider professional risk, think longer term, and explore opportunities for new personal career growth and development.

We chatted for a while longer and ended the call.

I called my brother. We talked a little and I shared my take-aways from the conversation with my boss.

Gerald suggested that I would have to make a difficult personal and professional career decision, abide by that decision, and execute.

Debbie and I discussed this new turn of events.

The opportunity. The concept of working with and alongside Gerald, every day.

How might this work? What if it did not work out? What would be our plan B?

After much deliberation, we agreed that I would accept this new challenge.

A month later, we were in the car and on the road, heading back to Johannesburg.

Debbie, our baby, and I.

A new adventure!

*****

We already owned a small house in Johannesburg, but it was located quite some distance from the retail store. It was the first house we had purchased for our new, young family to live in prior to my J&J transfer to the east coast.

We moved back into this house once our tenant vacated.

I had learned to be a landlord during my time with Janssen-Cilag. I did not find the experience of being a landlord enjoyable and decided not to ever purchase residential property for commercial purposes.

My commute to work by car would be tough, but doable. There were no public transit options available.

Soon we relocated to be closer to work. Moving home was easy. By now, I was quite adept at moving about, and not hanging my hat in one place for too long.

This feature - I learned later - is also a Power Position.

It is called *mobility*. I would add this to my growing portfolio of Power Positions.

For example, if a business manager, peer, or colleague were to ask how we might be able to explore and conquer business opportunities in a foreign land... I would immediately play a mobility Power Positions card from the bottom of my deck.

Many people would not consider relocating for work.

I would be the opposite.

The contrarian.

I would be willing to go anywhere, conquer new challenges, accept risk... to benefit our business, my family, and myself.

Even today I view myself as a citizen of the world, able to go anywhere, work anywhere, win in every place.

Including where others feared to tread.

This mindset would prove to be particularly useful, about a decade later.

*****

But first, I had to learn an entirely new business.

For the past few years, my clients were predominantly medical doctors and institutional buyers, like hospital administrators or drug distribution companies.

As a rule, my clients were highly skilled professional people. White collar businesspeople. Self-employed medical doctors. Even my employees were registered nurses, pharmacists, educated professionals. Business-to-Business (B2B) professionals.

Many young people spend a few years working in a Business-to-Consumer (B2C) environment during their high school and college years. I too had some of this experience, but mine was dated and limited to working the cash register at a supermarket... now already a decade prior.

My challenges included learning about unpredictable retail client behavior, the ebb and flow of sales revenue and customer foot traffic without any obvious logic or pattern, making ongoing adjustments from relatively formal B2B practices to accommodate the randomness of B2C... along with getting to grips with the tracking of day-to-day cash flow, inventory management, unique client requests, staying up to date on product innovation, etc.

At Johnson & Johnson I had learned and practiced The Pareto principle. This is colloquially known as the 80/20 rule.

It really is the law of the vital few, or the principle of factor sparsity. Many people will understand that for many events, roughly 80% of the effects come from 20% of the causes.

For example, in my previous job I was able to predict quite confidently - or forecast for financial purposes - that 80% of our sales would be generated from 20% of our customers.

Retail turns the Pareto principle upside-down. For example, 20% of the staff - on any given day - might generate 80% of the day's revenue. Until the next day when it would be the other way around. Or 20% of the customers accounted for 80% of the revenue, but without any predictability as to who the customers would be, when they would decide to make their purchases, and so on.

B2C is a tough business!

I greatly admire successful retailers. Even the greatest retail businesspeople, like Jeff Bezos from Amazon, must generate additional margin from revenue sources other than their primary, low-margin retail enterprises.

Amazon sells Prime membership subscriptions, they earn commission from sellers using their reseller website, they own Amazon Web Services (AWS), drive additional margin via fulfillment services and related logistics for their resellers, etc.

These are just some of the methodologies Bezos employs to help generate revenue of about $350,000 per employee, annually (2019).

Customers would come and go daily.

Randomly.

I do not like random.

I like organization, logic, rationalization, and a little luck.

More like backgammon.

Less like *Moksha Patam*, an ancient Indian board game more commonly known as *Snakes & Ladders* in English speaking countries.

I needed to adapt. And suddenly I needed to become intimately familiar with cash flow.

I had mentioned cash flow earlier. Author and real estate investor, Robert Kiyosaki, provided my first introduction to the four words every entrepreneur needed to know: assets, liabilities, and cash flow.

I would later spend time unlearning my accounting knowledge about assets and liabilities from my past, formal studies.

Nearly everything they had taught me in accounting classes at high school and university was wrong. Or at the very least, not applicable in real life, or business.

For now, cash flow would be king.

I had also previously learned that when a client interviewed a prospective accountant, one needed to ask the philosophical question, "What is 1 + 1?"

The correct answer from a skilled, potential CFO is, "What would you like it to be?"

Accounting is nuanced, not an absolute science.

*****

Slowly but surely, my brother who had previously been my

enemy… became my mentor.

I learned, over time, that his upbringing mirrored mine.

In fact, because he had spent more time in the presence of my father, he may have had an upbringing even worse than mine.

To this end, Gerald's ability to be financially self-sufficient, create sustainable business practices, dream up innovative ways to attract new business, while juggling and self-financing the cash flow demands of a growing business… collectively set me up properly for life's future adventures.

One day, he asked me whether I understood the difference between a markup and a margin. "Of course, I do", came my response, without even thinking.

He then challenged me quite simply with this question, "If I used a 10% markup and offered a client a 10% discount, how much profit would I make?"

Without hesitation, I confidently said, "Zero".

It was at the end of a day's work. Gerald suggested that I should think about that, and we would revisit the same question the next day.

I was a university level Accountancy major.

What a joke!

At least they taught us the double-entry accounting system. This was thought to have been invented by an Italian priest, Luca Pacioli, after he had written a book that is generally referred to as the "accounting bible".

Anyhow, by the next day, I knew the difference between a markup and a margin.

*****

CHAPTER 5

FINANCIAL LITERACY 101

Gerald and I worked together, or more specifically, together in the same place for about 4 years. During this time, we became good business partners.

Our respective skills were complementary. I was outgoing and salesy, good with clients. Gerald was always studious and acted like a patriarch, the guy in charge, the boss.

Business was good.

Success, unlike failure, is a poor teacher.

Gerald wanted to focus on a new wholesale venture. I was disinterested. He was confident that he had spotted a unique business opportunity. As is always the case, the best business opportunities are based on need, or consumer demand.

Gerald noticed that large U.S. corporations, including our vendors - like Kodak - were withdrawing from doing business in South Africa.

It is not so much that Kodak - a market leader at the time on the entire African continent - had arrived at a *come to Jesus* moment of their own, but rather that U.S. government sanctions had caused businesses to stop doing business in South Africa because of *apartheid*.

Legislated racial segregation policies were, and still are, offensive to most people. Of course, the United States had only ended its racial segregation policies a few years earlier, but it now successfully marketed itself as the *world's policeman* in the justifiable global fight against apartheid.

Uninformed people believed that sanctions would work and force change.

People who rely on the mainstream media for their world education are fabulously uninformed.

They would not know this, because it is exceedingly difficult for anyone to know what they do not know.

So, while the U.S. government and its propaganda division (a few owners of the cable and printed news networks), all touted the success of America's sanctions against South Africa, business continued as before, but just executed *differently*.

*****

How does sanctions-busting work?

For my example, I will use an imaginary U.S. corporation called ABC.

Someone innovative, like Gerald, created a new local business that would import ABC's *sanctioned products* from various third-party distributors located in another country, or multiple countries.

These global distributors were known by any name, other than ABC.

Any name, for example, *Bester Global*. ABC would knowingly

supply products to Bester Global.

Knowingly because Bester Global would suddenly start submitting purchase orders to sub-distributors that reflected a continuation of ABC's business in a particular jurisdiction. Business owners always know who and where their largest customers are.

For business of that magnitude, ABC would not only know the reason for the spike in business by the new market entrant, but also support Bester Global in many ways. In fact, they might even have created the new entity.

ABC would offer very favorable payment and settlement terms, low interest purchase financing, bulk order discounts, shipping and/or logistics support, etc.

ABC might co-invest in new warehousing, provide settlement kickbacks and/or cash incentives for capital expenditures (Capex), create unique/special packaging denoting different countries of origin for fast moving consumer goods (FMCG) categories, and more.

An executive officer or a few senior managers might "quit" their jobs as employees of ABC in the USA to go and work for Bester Global in another country.

Payroll costs for these new *Bester Global employees* might be borne by ABC itself, in a series of anonymous financial transactions that would compensate Bester Global for the newly incurred staff expenses.

You get the idea?

Gerald spotted the sanctions-busting business opportunity early and executed effectively, efficiently, and professionally.

Very soon, his new wholesale business started selling sanctioned American and European products to South African retail clients.

In this sense, I became my brother's client.

In the meantime, U.S. elected government officials rejoiced and patted themselves on the back.

They were enjoying the imaginary success of their sanctions imposed against the evil South African regime, with its racist segregation policies.

The intent was good, the execution entirely absent. They would be none the wiser, ignorant as they were regarding macroeconomic matters outside of their own country's borders.

By way of a real example, Delta Motor Corporation - a South African car manufacturer - was created through a management buy-out after General Motors (GM) divested from South Africa in 1986. It was headed by former GM executive, Bob Price, who had transferred to South Africa from Detroit.

*****

Gerald was now spending his days at his wholesale business, and I was spending mine at our retail businesses which had also expanded beyond our original single-location business.

Slowly, we were seeing one another less and less. But we would speak on the telephone often, as business partners in multiple business locations tend to do.

From time to time, he would chastise me for servicing or selling to his wholesale clients from our retail businesses.

Stealing his clients!

In turn, I would reply with something snarky like, "One shouldn't cannibalize your one business, to grow your other business!"

We were both competitive, and equally stubborn.

Gerald was older, and the majority shareholder. He would therefore typically win most business arguments. At the time, I had only acquired 10% equity in our original retail store, and 50% equity in another.

Over time, our business relationship became increasingly more strained. Ironically, at this time, our personal relationship had grown to be quite strong and enduring.

Most of the time, we agreed that any of our differences were just business, and not personal.

We co-existed and operated in this manner for a few more years before I asked him to exit his ownership of our jointly owned businesses. That way, I suggested he would be able to focus on his wholesale business and I would be able to shift my focus entirely to retail.

He agreed.

Sometime during 1994, and after having been business partners for about six years, my brother and I ended our everyday working relationship and formal business partnership.

I acquired the 90% ownership that Gerald held in our original business with the help of a business partner and purchased the 50% equity he owned in our second retail operation, outright.

Effectively, I now owned 50% of one retail operation, and 100% of the other. Gerald, in turn, owned 100% of his wholesale venture.

We remained reasonably close as friends until 1998, when my family and I departed South Africa for immigration to Canada.

I did not have many opportunities to thank him for his mentorship during the earlier part of my professional career.

Later, on more than one occasion, I reminded him that he was one of my heroes.

*****

By the mid-nineties, Debbie and I had two young sons.

Our second child was born in 1993.

Debbie and I started working together on a different exit strategy.

This time, we were planning to exit South Africa.

Its general lawlessness was often accompanied by violence. Almost everyone we knew had been touched by some form of crime or violent actions directly, in South Africa.

Violence and economic disruption had directly impacted our family too.

On one occasion, several armed burglars entered our home at around 3 AM despite armed security systems and posted warnings that an armed company would respond if our alarms were triggered.

On this occasion, Debbie and our two young sons huddled in our *safe room* while I started firing a few shots at the burglars with a .38 special revolver.

When I started shooting, the hoodlums scrambled, and fled.

The safe room was a relatively large walk-in closet with a sheet of metal on the inside of the door. Inside that closet we had a large, heavy rifle safe that housed another few guns and some ammunition. Fortunately, Debbie did not have to use any of our hidden extra firepower to defend herself and our two young sons!

We had suffered other instances of direct violence too, at our businesses and our family home.

This was our primary driver for our new mission...

Leaving South Africa.

*****

In a way, our immigration planning had started in 1991.

During June of that year, I had an opportunity to spend time in training at the Leica factory located in Wetzlar, Germany. For people in the know, Leitz - or Leica as it became known later - is a manufacturer of the finest optical lenses, scopes, and cameras on the planet.

While learning about Leica cameras, it dawned upon me that I was uniquely positioned to turn a handsome profit from this endeavor. My shops sold used cameras, and we frequently received older Leica cameras with various lenses as trade-ins. Some were estate sales, or sometimes just people trying to sell grandpa's old camera they had accidentally discovered in the basement.

The interesting twist to the business opportunity was that European collectors attached greater value to vintage Leica products. As a result, they were willing to pay much higher prices than their South African peers.

Upon my return to Johannesburg from Wetzlar, I searched for, and then sourced a potential reseller in Europe. I had a friend in Zurich. I asked him whether he would be able to resell some Leica cameras for me in exchange for a commission.

He did a little homework and connected with the owner of a reputable photographic store in Zurich. An expert Leica specialist dealer, like my businesses in South Africa.

I would source Leica products in South Africa, for us to resell in Zurich. We all understood that sourcing would be random and unpredictable, but also that the cost of the products would be reasonably low, compared with the potential future resale value.

I set about purchasing any used Leica products I was able to source from clients in South Africa. I paid them cash in local currency. Then, I sent the products to my friend in Zurich, via airmail. He delivered the cameras to the local Leica dealer for resale.

We offered the Swiss retail store owner a great deal: nominally, my asking price in Swiss Franc (CHF) was more-or-less the same price I had paid for the goods in South African rand (ZAR).

By way of a simple example, if I had purchased a camera for ZAR100 I offered it to the reseller for CHF100.

But at the time, the currency exchange rate was approximately CHF1 = ZAR5.

This exchange rate delivered an immediate 5x return on the purchase price, in local currency, but before taking any costs like shipping into consideration.

Once the products were sold my friend trimmed his 10% commission of the top of our share of the sales price. Then he deposited the remaining balance into my local bank account, in Zurich.

I obviously incurred costs. Some were *hard costs*, like packaging and shipping. Others were more figurative or *soft costs*, like the time value of money related to the time of purchase vs. the time of resale.

Additional costs included servicing and/or repairs as required, discounts when offered, and commissions paid to the two resellers.

Yet additional expenses included indirect or unpredictable costs, like product returns, lost packages, defective products, etc.

If I were to factor all the above into my overall cost of doing this business the real profits were negligible, despite the 5x initial return on the prevailing exchange rate at the time.

In the greater scheme of things, I might have managed to *break even* most of the time.

But I was not doing these transactions to generate a profit, let alone an ongoing income.

It was an asset relocation exercise. Effectively, I was transferring after-tax, earned income from South Africa to a foreign domiciled bank.

*****

Some of my wealthier clients were more creative.

Their movable assets sometimes included a boat or a small aircraft.

Assets that could easily be relocated or transported to another city, in another country, and sold at that destination. Even at a loss.

But payment for the transaction would once again be received in the local currency of that particular jurisdiction. And that payment received in exchange for the asset would then be deposited in an offshore bank account, elsewhere.

For example, one could fly a small aircraft to another country, sell it upon arrival, and bank the cash locally.

The seller would pay for his expenses including meals, accommodation, and airfare to get back home with a credit card. That way, the proceeds of his sale was deposited in full, while the balance due on the credit card transactions would be settled later, back home, using domestic currency.

It is important to mention that government taxes are levied on income earned.

The transactions described here illustrate the movement or transfer of fiat currency, rather than income earned.

These business deals were unlikely to create tax events because there would be either no income earned (i.e., no profit), or the assets described might have been sold for a net loss.

Some people took far greater risks.

One of my clients used to visit war torn areas in Central Africa from time to time to purchase diamonds.

Uncut.

And then, via some interesting back channels, he would either sell them to international diamond dealers or barter them in exchange for things that he might have needed for himself.

Blood Diamonds?

One day, he visited and inquired about a new professional Nikon camera he was after. We had one available in our inventory on hand. He produced a small tobacco pouch from his pocket. It contained several small stones, that he described as uncut diamonds.

He asked whether I would accept some gems in exchange for the camera. I declined. I would not know whether the gems were diamonds or not. And anyway, I would not know what to do with the diamonds afterwards, assuming they were real.

Politicians create restrictive laws, often with good intent – dictating what ordinary people are allowed to do with their earned, after-tax money - and smart people generally figure out ways to circumvent those laws.

Taxes are levied on earned income.

If one does not generate taxable income - which is no different from electing not to sell publicly traded stocks for realized gains - no tax events are created.

During one of the 2016 presidential debates between Donald Trump and Hillary Clinton, she accused him of not having paid any taxes, or otherwise not paying his *fair share*.

His response?

Something like, "That means I'm smart." Then he added, "And, by the way, I did not write the tax laws, you guys did."

This last statement was mostly true.

Clinton and her husband were political lifers.

Trump, on the other hand, was the proverbial new kid on the block, in political context.

*****

Some of the stories shared above may sound like scenes from a movie, but the sum of the parts is relatively simple.

The back story is that the South African government, at the time, had restrictions that prohibited or limited citizens from taking after-tax currency out of the country.

But there were fewer restrictions on goods and services, especially small, random lots of relatively inexpensive, used cameras.

South Africans were also somewhat restricted from owning foreign bank accounts without the local central bank's permission.

An example of an exemption from this restriction was a business engaged in import and export of commercial goods. I owned multiple businesses, doing just that.

Business owners effectively had little choice, but to open and operate bank accounts in foreign jurisdictions. And most international trade was - and still is - settled in U.S. dollars.

Rand, the local South African currency, was too volatile to risk exchange rate fluctuations on international trade orders.

Buying forward cover was prohibitively expensive for the same reason.

Furthermore, the Rand had virtually zero value outside of Southern Africa... save for in neighboring countries, like Namibia, Botswana, and Zimbabwe.

As the owner of businesses doing international trade, obtaining permission for a foreign bank account was a relative formality.

It required a completed application, a processing fee (tax), and a signature and rubber stamp from a government clerk.

One could expedite the processing of most government applications for licenses for token gratuity amounts paid to the processing clerk, e.g., R100 cash.

Of course, Switzerland had no such restrictions or laws. It marketed Zurich as the banking capital of the world.

New York, Hong Kong, and London... eat your hearts out!

*****

That Swiss Bank Account?

I had been saving up some cash for the proverbial rainy day.

Then one day, prior to leaving for a business trip to Europe, I purchased an international bank draft at my local bank in South Africa, for CHF10,000.

That was the maximum foreign currency withdrawal amount allowed an adult citizen (at the time) for any personal use, not including family vacation allowance.

On that trip, one weekday morning, I arrived at Zurich's main station by train from the airport.

I exited the station onto Hauptbahnhof Strasse, a busy main street directly in front of the Central Station, and walked a few blocks down the street doing a visual reconnaissance.

The Union Bank of Switzerland (UBS) appeared to be the largest bank building, and most visible in terms of its footprint and branding on that busy street.

I entered the bank's lobby and asked a friendly young lady at a customer service desk whether I would be able to open a personal, non-resident banking account.

She directed me to an account manager who opened an account for me. I offered my international bank draft as a means of funding the new account.

The account manager informed me that it would take about 30 days for a South African bank draft to clear. The funds would be available for withdrawal sometime in the future. I was fine with that.

The entire process was as simple as described above.

In addition to my overseas business accounts, I was now the proud owner of a personal Swiss bank account. That may sound impressive but do keep in mind that my account had a humble balance of CHF10,000.

I was not the typical high roller one might imagine.

Especially when romanticizing Swiss bank accounts.

*****

Within a few months, my bank balance started growing in dribs and drabs, especially because I did not make any withdrawals.

Every few weeks or months, I would ship a small carton of used Leica cameras to my friend in Zurich. And a few weeks later he would make a relatively small deposit into my local bank account in Zurich. My balance just kept ticking over, slowly.

Products purchased in ZAR, sold in CHF.

You might wonder why I would even explore this transfer of fiat currency. The answer is quite simple: I was laying the foundation for a future exit from South Africa... to parts unknown.

This, and our local currency was devaluing rapidly against major foreign currencies. An investment into nearly any other, stable, and more secure currency created a hedge against our local decline in buying power, and general wealth.

I was now learning forex hedging.

*****

CHAPTER 6

ALL IN THE FAMILY

Life was mostly normal in South Africa, often mundane.

Most dinner-table conversations centered around emigration, local politics, crime, and sporting events.

Almost everyone knew someone who had been a victim, directly impacted by rampant crime and lawlessness.

Our family members perhaps had a car stolen, a burglary at home, or been victims of a *hijacking*. The latter became the default verbiage for car theft at gunpoint, a common crime in South Africa.

Almost everyone we knew was either planning to leave the country themselves or knew someone who was planning to leave the country.

Of my siblings, at that time, only my brother Abe and I were planning to leave. But much of the family talk was ongoing mumbling and grumbling, caused by fear and uncertainty about everyone's respective futures.

A few years later, Debbie and I would leave South Africa.

Of our family peers we were the first emigrants. Abe and his family followed shortly thereafter. My sister Maggie and her husband also eventually left a few years later.

Gerald remained in South Africa until he died in 2014.

Abe and Maggie - along with their respective families - later returned to South Africa for reasons best known to them.

Debbie and I elected to rebuild our lives in Canada, where we lived for about a decade. Later, we relocated to the United States.

I have not written much about my siblings, other than my brother Gerald, and my sister Maggie.

That is mainly because Gerald had also been my business partner for nearly a decade. And he and his family were located - geographically - nearest to Debbie and me.

*****

I admire my two other brothers - Abe, and Sean - for different reasons.

Abe is one of the brightest, smartest, and most studious people I have ever had the pleasure of spending time with. He is also extraordinarily kind and generous.

And, of all my family members - excluding my time spent working with Gerald - Abe is the sibling I have connected and kept in contact with more than the others.

Sean was dealt a horrible hand in terms of his entry into adulthood. A losing rather than a winning hand, dealt from a proverbial bottom of life's deck of cards.

Earlier, when I shared the story about my mother's passing, I mentioned that I was nearly 13 years old at the time of her death. At that time, Sean was about to turn 18. His birth date was the day before mine, but I was five years younger.

Losing one's mother is probably tough at any age? Sean's age at that time would prove this loss particularly difficult.

We - Sean and I, more so than our siblings - had been raised by a single, working mother.

In the absence of a father or another adult capable of providing mentorship, discipline, financial, and supervisory support... the untimely passing of our mother grossly exacerbated our already dire circumstances.

Earlier, I briefly mentioned that Sean had been accepted into the police college for training as a cadet. That meant he would receive free room and board, regular meals, and clothing for work purposes during his basic training.

My story ignores any time-related gaps between our mother's passing and Sean's acceptance into the police training college.

Where was he *in-between* these macro life events?

Contrast this with my own experiences shared above. At least I remember my own circumstances and movements immediately following my mother's passing, or my departure from Gerald's house the day after writing my final high school examination paper and then starting at university in a different city, two months later.

Life does not happen in some organized, arranged fashion. Personally, I can account for most of my whereabouts at the time, from memory, but I am unable to speak for my siblings.

Unpredictable events happen when one least expects it. And every story has a beginning, middle, and an end. It is easy to gloss over the middle part, which is often the most interesting, daunting, or captivating part of a story.

I am not going to dwell on this topic, because I cannot do it justice. I will only add that Maggie and her husband were incredibly helpful during a time when Abe, Sean, and I (later, after having left Gerald's house), needed any help.

This is true in more ways that I could possibly describe.

Due to circumstances, my siblings and I never really had much opportunity to spend time together.

For periods of time - for example when I lived and later worked with Gerald - the two of us had some familial connectivity.

But my four siblings and I only very rarely saw one another or just visited one another, as families often tend to do.

Most often, the periods of time that passed between us having an opportunity to get together as a family spanned several years.

*****

While I spent my teenage years living with Gerald in Cape Town; Maggie lived in a small town east of Johannesburg; Abe was at university studying law in Port Elizabeth; and Sean was a police constable, near Pretoria.

These four cities above are in different parts of the country, hours apart by plane, let alone by car or rail.

Occasionally, we would have opportunities to meet up. This was generally necessitated because of some bad news, like when Ouma died.

Or when our father died, we were all able to attend his funeral. This moment in my life had a profound effect on my mental state.

At the time of our father's funeral, three of my older siblings - Gerald, Maggie, and Sean - were already somewhat mature and settled, for the most part. They were married, had children, a place to live, owned their own cars, etc.

Abe was a mature and independent student, a young man quite capable of taking care of himself.

But I literally had nothing.

It was the loneliest period of my life. At the time of my father's death, I was working at the Holiday Inn.

The hotel offered some perks to a young employee, like uniforms (that were regularly laundered by the hotel's housekeeping staff), free meals from a restaurant's buffet during working shifts, and even an occasional room to use e.g., for a nap between back-to-back shifts.

Excluding these useful benefits, I literally owned nothing other than some personal items like clothing and a sponge mattress on the floor of the small apartment I was renting, directly across the street from the Holiday Inn hotel where I worked.

After my father's funeral, my siblings and I scattered back to our respective hideaways.

Them, to their homes with their respective families.

Me, to my cobbled-together domicile described above.

Alone. Lonely. Directionless.

*****

But there were also happy times.

Sometimes, three or four of us would manage to get together for a celebratory purpose, someone's birthday, or a Christmas lunch.

Still, hardly ever, would all five siblings be together in one place, at one time.

Even as I write this, I have not seen Maggie or Sean for more than a decade. Abe and I have managed to meet up during various international travels. Gerald died in 2014.

It should therefore not seem too unusual for me to describe my wife and two sons as my family, often neglecting to mention my siblings.

*****

At the start of this chapter I wrote, "I admire my two brothers, Abe and Sean, for very different reasons."

I will briefly explain.

Abe self-financed and successfully completed one of the toughest and demanding academic programs at university, at the time. He graduated, joined a law firm as an article clerk, and worked to gain admission to the bar as a practicing lawyer.

He decided to specialize in Intellectual Property. Later, he was called to the bar as an advocate of the Supreme Court of South Africa.

An advocate - also called a Queen's Counsel (or QC) in many Commonwealth jurisdictions - appears only in the highest court of the country, on behalf of a client.

As a *specialist lawyer*, an advocate's client is the lawyer who is representing either a defendant or plaintiff.

Abe had achieved professional success because of his superior intelligence, general knowledge about diverse subject matters, sheer grit and determination, personal ethics, time management... and many, many hours of hard work!

*****

I have a unique, albeit distant, affinity for Sean.

This is mainly because during most of the time we were homeless, we were together.

From the time my father walked out the door - I was 5, and Sean 10 years old - we lived in various places with my mother until the day she died about 8 years later.

I shared that Sean had been accepted into police college as a trainee cadet. Post-graduation, he was posted to a local police station, in Pretoria, to work as a police constable.

He married his first wife at a young age. Much like Sean, she was also young and immature. They had two children within the first couple of years of their marriage.

Sean was a young, immature, poorly compensated, rookie police constable with a stay-at-home wife and two young children.

What could possibly go wrong?

Just in terms of the brief comments shared above one can easily imagine their challenging circumstances.

The *Police* provided budget accommodation for cops with families.

My brother and his wife were two young parents poorly equipped for adulthood, never mind parenthood.

Two little children exacerbated their financial woes and strained relationship.

Survival.

Not a great start in life.

But survive, they did!

Sean later left the police force, and then tried every imaginable job to sustain himself and his family financially.

He would later drift from one job to another, perhaps in search of a dream job. He would also drift from one wife to another, perhaps in search of a dream girl?

But, in his late 40's - with financial assistance provided mostly by Abe - Sean went *back to school*. He was probably the most senior and oldest law school graduate in his cohort when he matriculated a few years later.

In the context of *it is never too late*, I can only offer that regardless of what had happened before, Sean successfully qualified as a lawyer.

A few years later, he too hung out a shingle and opened his own legal practice.

He once joked that his clients would often approach him with problems that they believe are unique to themselves: "My wife wants a divorce". "My business is going under". "I am being sued for…"

Sean would then be able to respond with something like, "I've been there a few times myself. Let's discuss your situation and your available options".

Heroes, for different reasons.

*****

CHAPTER 7

OH CANADA!

Debbie and I applied for Canadian permanent residency status in 1997.

As was my custom, I requested the application forms from the Canadian Consulate in Pretoria, South Africa, and personally completed our application.

My practice and habits in this regard might seem a little odd. Even miserly. After all, I could have afforded to hire an immigration lawyer to do the administrivia for me.

But my approach to this concept is rather simple.

A lawyer doing the work on my behalf would need to gather all the information required for my application, from my family and myself.

This literally means we would need to first gather and then organize that information before forwarding it to the lawyer. Then, the lawyer would need to enter the data that I had provided, and I would again need to review the completed forms to ensure that the information - as presented - matched my original submission, etc.

This implies that I would be required to do most of the work myself, twice!

And then I would have to wait for the lawyer to file my application.

In about the same amount of time it would have taken me to find and secure the services of a good immigration lawyer... I personally completed the steps mentioned above, submitted the application, paid the required fees... and then joined the queue of applicants patiently awaiting the processing of their permanent residency applications.

Abe would be horrified at my amateurish, lackadaisical approach to a matter of such great importance!

*****

It took two years for the Canadian High Commission in Pretoria to process our application.

During that time, my family and I visited Canada twice.

In 1997 Debbie and I, along with our two young sons, visited Toronto, Canada for a few weeks. We were doing reconnaissance as soon-to-be new permanent residents.

On several occasions I asked my family, "Could you live here? And "Do you think you might like to live here?"

Their feedback was positive, exciting, and even hopeful.

In 1998 we visited again. This time we invited Debbie's parents to join us.

We wanted to create an opportunity for them to personally see, and experience Toronto and surrounding cities like Niagara Falls.

*****

South Africa had various foreign currency restrictions in place, as I had shared previously.

These restrictions limited the amount of local currency a person was legally allowed to withdraw for personal use, like an overseas vacation, annually.

Additional travelers increased that total travel currency allowance significantly.

The annual limits were quite generous, rather than restrictive. In 1997, it was ZAR100,000 per adult traveler.

Two adults traveling would be double that amount. Minors traveling with their parents had smaller travel allowances.

A family travel allowance for four average-income, working people added up to a large amount of money.

For sure, the travel allowances were greater than what most working people could afford, especially for discretionary spending purposes like an overseas holiday.

In 1997 our total travel allowance was ZAR250,000.

We were unable to set aside that much money, but during the years prior we had squirreled away as much savings as we were able to afford.

The following year Debbie's parents joined us, nearly doubling that travel allowance. It was completely beyond our reach in terms of cash on hand plus savings.

I am sharing this information because we would have been able to withdraw a relatively large amount of cash for travel purposes, and deposit it elsewhere.

If only we had that much cash!

Regardless of how much money we were able to set aside, we viewed the trips as all-expenses-paid-locally.

Our mindset was that we were embarking on these trips for personal learning, exploration, and pleasure… but also to deposit savings in Canada, for our future use.

If our application for residency were rejected for whatever reason, I could always transfer our cash elsewhere.

Effectively, our *annual holiday travel allowance* constituted cash transferred to an offshore bank account legally, and it would immediately be available for our use once we arrived as permanent residents.

I had no reason to believe that our permanent residency application would not be approved. We had already qualified under the category I had selected. And our interviews with Canadian High Commission staffers in Pretoria had been completed without any hiccups.

We meticulously prepared a travel budget. I prepaid our travel, accommodation, and car rental expenses locally, using domestic currency.

Then we purchased Canadian currency with whatever amount of local currency we had left over. From this amount we estimated what we would need to spend daily in Canada while on vacation, and we added the remaining balance to our anticipated budget amount for deposit into our Canadian bank account.

Our foreign currency purchases were recorded as annual travel allowance allocations. The selling bank was responsible for with recording and remitting the relevant paperwork to the authorities.

The bank also recorded and entered the amount of foreign currency purchased into our passports, and *rubber-stamped* it, as was the custom at the time.

Once in Toronto, on vacation, we used cash sparingly, spending mostly using credit cards. The credit card debt could be settled back home again in local currency. This is an important point. It allowed us to purchase foreign currency using our travel allowance, and deposit that money overseas.

By doing so, we avoided using much of the foreign currency, squirrelling most of it away into a Canadian bank account.

We repeated the same process one more time, early in 1999, when we traveled to Toronto on vacation with one-way tickets.

During the two years preceding our departure from South Africa, we were able to legally withdraw a relatively large amount of our personal savings. We effectively deposited that portion of our savings into a new, non-resident checking account at the Bank of Montreal, in Toronto.

In 1999 the currency exchange rate was about CAD$1 = ZAR3.00. At the time of writing the exchange rate was about CAD$1 = ZAR12. You can do the math!

We *moved money* as part of our relocation planning and created a hedge against the rapidly declining local currency.

We managed to accumulate and save a humble, yet sizable sum of cash - relatively speaking - for our family to deploy while we set about planning our new lives in a foreign country.

I had filed my Canadian permanent residency application as a *self-employed entrepreneur*.

This status or category - once approved - would require me to create a new business, employment for Canadians, and/or invest in an existing business in Canada.

We waited... but kept ourselves busy.

*****

I executed a few final business transactions before we departed South Africa for good.

I informed my staff that my family and I were planning to leave the country.

We offered them very favorable terms to acquire our retail businesses, for example, no initial cash investment and flexible repayment terms over periods they would be comfortable with.

Our final offer was simple:

We would only withdraw my original cash investments (or initial owner's equity). All cash remaining after that withdrawal would be left in the business as working capital for them to use to pay the rent, purchase products, settle supplier accounts, etc.

The businesses had no long-term debt obligations, making the purchase offer even sweeter.

I wanted to reward them because, after all, they had helped us to build the businesses into successful, financially self-sustaining entities… that had supported our family and theirs, respectively, for nearly ten years.

I elected to forego complex valuation methodologies - like discounted cash flow modeling - to estimate the value of our business entities.

I also did not attach or apply multiples to common metrics like annual revenue or net income, as would be custom for owners considering an exit or divestiture of business interests to external buyers.

I was already financially secure and not motivated by greed. It would now be their opportunity to build some personal wealth.

It was indeed a sweet deal for my staff, but they were more like family than employees.

I did add one additional provision to our sales agreements. We agreed that if they generated a net profit beyond a certain hurdle rate we had agreed upon - during only their first year of ownership - I would be entitled to 15% of that net profit, in full and final settlement.

As it turned out, they were not able to exceed that hurdle rate and I did not receive any further payment. My financial exit as described above constituted the full value of my business disposition.

We sold our family home, which was mortgaged, and used a portion of the profit derived from that sale to rent a small apartment. We lived in a 2-bedroom apartment for a few months until we were legally allowed to emigrate to Canada, as permanent residents.

We had also owned two luxury vehicles. Two BMW sedans that were jointly worth quite a large sum of money in local terms. In South Africa, cars are expensive!

I sold one car to a cash buyer and bartered the other.

This bartering transaction was a swap of the car plus a relatively small amount of cash in exchange for a 40' container of photographic accessory products manufactured in Taiwan.

The manufacturer of the products was a South African permanent resident, and a close friend.

He gave the car to his wife and allocated the cash portion of our exchange to the cost of production of the goods he would manufacture and later ship to me, to Canada.

This physical transfer of assets allowed me to use local currency and a vehicle to pay for a container of goods.

The total deal value at the time was about ZAR50,000. Converted, this container of goods would add about CAD$15,000 worth of relocated assets to our pool of resources.

But the actual value of the products could prove to be much higher.

CAD$15,000 represented the cost of the manufactured goods, or cost of goods sold (COGS), sometime in the future. I was already intimately familiar with COGS because of my retail experience.

I knew I would be able to sell the goods at a wholesale value of perhaps 2-3x the landed cost. I planned to start a wholesale business rather than going back into retail.

The 40' container of goods could potentially generate about CAD $30,000-45,000 in gross revenue. All I had to do was incorporate a company and find customers to purchase my products.

I did both.

But shortly after our arrival in Canada in 1999 the photographic accessories market imploded due to the rapid adoption of digital photography. As you might imagine, a small digital camera no longer required the use of a *gadget bag* for lenses and flashguns, a tripod for still shots, a variety of photographic lenses and filters, and so on.

But I managed to sell most of the products over time. Initially, I positioned my new company as a wholesaler and sold the products to retail shops. Eventually, I managed to clear the last remaining items to a cash wholesale distribution business, in Montreal.

The container load of photographic accessory products, all being said, probably generated an amount just slightly greater than my initial cost. At least we did not lose any money. That was despite the market collapse cause by the shift from film cameras and cassette tape camcorders to digital photography.

At around the same time, I learned about Warren Buffet's two rules for people who manage *other people's money*.

Going forward, I would adopt these as part of my personal money management strategy.

The rules are:

1. Do not lose money.
2. Do not forget rule 1.

*****

In November 1998 we received notification that our permanent residency applications for migration to Canada had been approved. But as you can probably tell from the story told thus far, we had been at the ready for quite some time.

By waiting until January 1999 to depart, we were able to withdraw foreign currency using our family travel allowance for that new year once again, entirely legally.

It was a new fiscal year. We had already used our family holiday allowance for the previous year, as described earlier, and annual travel allowances did not carry forward from year to year.

To this end, we were able to pool the cash from all the transactions mentioned above and withdraw another family vacation allowance to add to our Canadian cash float.

During our last month in South Africa, we shipped a few personal effects to Canada via ocean container, and purchased a few high-value portable products, like laptops and software, with local currency.

We donated whatever personal effects we could not carry - or anything that was going to be left behind - to family, friends, or charity.

We departed for Toronto from Johannesburg airport, via Frankfurt.

Upon arrival in Canada on January 4th, 1999, we were greeted by the largest snowstorm in Toronto's history.

In fact, that storm dumped so much snow onto Toronto that the mayor felt compelled to call a State of Emergency, and request deployment of the Canadian Armed Forces to assist city residents who were buried under twenty feet of snow.

Welcome to Canada!

*****

CHAPTER 8

BLUE JAYS, RAPTORS, MAPLE LEAFS, BAD COFFEE AND CANADIAN BEER

My family and I started assimilating, attempting to become more Canadian, from day one.

We learned the words of the national anthem; attended Blue Jays baseball, Raptors basketball, and Maple Leafs hockey games; drank local beer and Tim Horton's coffee; and started meeting and spending time with new friends.

We explored nearby Ontario cities, and larger cities in the province next door, Quebec. Meeting polite, friendly Canadians nearly everywhere we visited.

Later, I would learn that Amazon founder and businessman extraordinaire, Jeff Bezos, had a philosophy that every day was Day One. I shamelessly stole that concept.

What a great way to view every new day!

*****

We had initially moved into a furnished apartment at Yonge-Eg-linton, an upscale neighborhood in Toronto. We had not planned it that way, but it rather just happened to be where our apartment was located.

I had booked and prepaid the apartment rental for two months before leaving South Africa. That way we had an address to go to upon arrival and some sense of stability for the first few weeks.

We lived at that apartment until the end of February.

During those first weeks we purchased a new Ford Escort station wagon, a reliable small car. We created and set up internet and email accounts for news and communication, purchased insurance, applied for Ontario driver's licenses and Canadian Health Cards, learned about the schooling systems and its daily routines, and more.

We were settling in.

A short while later we had a business registered, and I awaited a container of products to offer for sale to Canadian photographic and electronic retailers.

Canadians are nice people. They are generally friendly and very polite.

The kids started school. Debbie and I stayed home. We wrote emails about our adventures to our family back home and in other countries. We went shopping for things we needed, explored potential markets and clients for our range of products that would be arriving soon, and went on lunch dates while the kids were at school.

In the evenings, unless there were blizzard conditions outside, we - as a family - would go for a short walk, stopping at kid-friendly restaurants and coffee shops, while discussing the day's activities and sharing our learnings about our new home and country.

During the day, Debbie and I also searched for a new, more permanent home.

On weekends, we started exploring the surrounding areas. Unless it was snowing because I had no experience driving a car in wintery conditions.

Fortunately, we did not have any more snow for a few weeks. It was just bitterly cold. Especially for a family of recent migrants from sunny South Africa!

We had left South Africa right at the peak of its typical warm summer and arrived in Canada in the middle of a winter season that seemed to be everlasting.

We had migrated from a city with average summer temperatures of around 82F/25C - with mostly sunny days and clear skies - to a city with an average winter temperature below freezing; grey, dull and overcast... and about 3 hours of daylight every day.

Suck it up, buttercups!

*****

Within a few weeks, we signed a lease for a 3-bedroom apartment in an area called Don Mills. This bedroom community is located about 10 miles northeast of downtown Toronto.

We chose the apartment and area because it was perfectly suited to our needs, the schools were nearby, and it was in a residential neighborhood. It would be better than living within the city with two young children.

The apartment was huge, because it also featured a full-sized, finished basement.

Initially, I considered using the basement for product storage. But anyone who has ever experienced the sheer bulk and volume of goods packed into a 40' container would understand that this idea was preposterous, to put it mildly. Renting some storage units nearby seemed to be a much better plan.

Our personal possessions arrived in Toronto before the ocean freight container of commercial products.

It had traveled from our home in Johannesburg, to Durban, to Rotterdam, and then to Montreal via a container ship, before arriving at our new home in Toronto. Not a single item had been damaged or broken. We were quite surprised!

A few weeks later the 40' container arrived, containing the products we had purchased from various factories in Taiwan.

We were in business, but without any clients.

I had studio pictures of some of the products ready for marketing purposes.

We had sold the same products in South Africa for many years. Therefore, the required ramp-up to learn to do business in Canada excluded a usual requirement for a salesperson to become familiar with the business and/or its products.

We needed to find clients, figure out logistics, pricing, and distribution.

With my product photographs in hand, we hired someone to create a website for us. The website included an online store. Our business was expertly presented online, featuring professional quality product images. An online store with an interactive shopping cart was considered cutting edge and innovative in 1999!

I was stunned that not one single person went online to visit our website to place an order.

For perspective, the internet was "new". Amazon was a startup selling a few books online. No-one had informed me that people would not simply, miraculously, find a business online, and then start to purchase whatever goods they wanted.

But our website was so awesome?

I was convinced that online shopping would be a new way of doing business in the new century. This would prove to be correct. But we had a few *blind spots*, mostly related to a complete lack of understanding of how the internet worked, online marketing, generating clicks, etc.

My near-term solution to a lack of sales was probably a default action mimicking what most salespeople trained in the art of selling encyclopedias door-to-door would have done.

I created a catalogue using my product photographs, gathered a selection of sample products, purchased an order book... and went cold-calling on prospective clients. Now I was walking into a retail shop carrying a load of bags and accessories and asking to see the store manager, or buyer.

Many sophisticated retailers would ask whether I had arranged an appointment.

I had no idea that people managing a retail store would require a prospective vendor to make an appointment to discuss a business opportunity.

I had come to Canada from a less sophisticated business environment where people did silly things... like pick up and answer a phone when it rang; greeted and allocated time to people who arrived without an appointment and asked to see the manager; where people - in business - would not dare to eat their lunch or drink coffee in front of a customer or vendor; etc.

I had lots to learn!

But I was stubborn and persistent, and just kept hustling.

Some retailers would look at the products on offer, acknowledge that my deals, pricing and offers were great (good products offered by someone with near zero overhead cost), and place an order for their store.

Then, I would go to our storage units with our Ford station wagon, pack the order myself and deliver it the next day. I offered the retailers 30-day payment terms.

Many clients paid for their purchases within a reasonable period. Some did not. Yet others never paid. Eventually, some went out of business.

Chasing accounts receivables does not constitute time well spent. It is an activity that requires revisiting clients previously served - in an environment with unpleasant undertones - plus a loss of time that could have been spent more productively doing business elsewhere, instead.

I was learning that purchase orders for my products that were the easiest to secure... were ones from customers that I would be least happy about in the future, or that I should even have avoided in the first place.

What I mean by this statement above is simply this: where I walked into a retailer for the first time ever, exited with a sizable order in hand, and offered them 30-days to settle my invoice... it was easy because they were often more desperate than what I was, and they were probably going to go out of business soon.

Conversely, the harder I had to work to secure an order, and the longer it took for me to win the buyer's trust, the better my business' performance, based on the criteria above.

Some of my earliest and/or first customers went out of business, and I - like most vendors - lost money as an unsecured creditor. This experiment drives the cost of client acquisition and doing business sky-high.

Difficult customers were often the best customers, over time. They were generally managing their businesses professionally, treating their suppliers and employees with respect, they would examine products and/or each item meticulously before placing an order, and so on.

*****

While I was out selling, packing, and delivering photographic accessories, I was also scanning the market for jobs.

As a rule, Canadian salaries are high.

Employees - especially those working for larger corporations - are paid very well, despite working for the federal government for more than six months out of every year.

Canadian taxes are exceedingly high.

In addition to high personal income tax rates, Canadians also pay federal and provincial sales taxes.

The latter is a consumption tax, which is also high. In Ontario for example - the largest and wealthiest Canadian province - the Harmonized Sales Tax (federal and provincial) rate is 13%.

Marginal tax rates vary. A typical mid-level manager, for example, might have a marginal federal income tax rate of about 30%.

If one were to include the HST consumption tax mentioned above, the tax burden for this mid-level manager increases into the mid-40's instantly. And that would be before all other local or provincial taxes, property taxes, a relatively new Canadian carbon tax, and other *invisible* taxes like gasoline tax, etc.

This example above is why I referred to Canadians working for the federal government for six or more months out of every year.

It is probably more like seven or more months of taxes, subject to one's personal income tax bracket, and domicile for tax purposes.

A common Canadian counterargument to their high tax rates is *free healthcare*. Of course, there is no such thing as free healthcare, because healthcare - as a percentage of Canadian GDP - is the primary reason for the country's exorbitantly high tax rates!

Socialized healthcare is unfortunately one of those contentious issues where the government's intent is good, but the execution is sadly lacking.

A benefit of the government-run system - that cannot be disputed - is that no person should face financial ruin or bankruptcy because of their inability to pay for medical treatment when they are, or become, seriously ill.

This last point is a significant and unfortunate negative byproduct of America's (mostly) private-run healthcare systems. Issues like price-gouging, frivolous lawsuits, aggressive sales tactics and fear mongering by profit-hungry healthcare providers, high prescription medication prices, medical insurance price manipulation and fraud, etc., seriously damage the standing of the U.S. preferred *free-market* healthcare system.

During my decade spent living and working in Canada, I got to know the healthcare system quite well. I spent time volunteering at a local hospital and served on the board of directors for an in-home healthcare services provider.

I can confidently offer these observations about socialized healthcare, at a high level:

1. People do not receive exorbitantly priced hospital bills that they cannot afford to pay.
2. Generally, doctor's visits and any required hospitalization costs are covered.
3. The government plan does not cover out-of-pocket

expenses for necessary medical services like dentistry, vision, prescribed pharmaceuticals, etc. As a result, almost every employed Canadian contributes about the same - or even more than the average American payer - for top-up health insurance that covers these additional costs, via an employer sponsored private health insurance plan.

For example, my son and his family in Canada pay more for their top-up share of private healthcare insurance than what my spouse and I pay in the United States for our annual medical insurance plan.

However, for clarity, unlike our Canadian family members, we are required to pay the first US$8,500 out-of-pocket per person annually, before medical insurance coverage even begins.

One can purchase medical insurance plans with far lower deductibles, but at much higher prices. We can afford to accommodate and accept this level of coverage mentioned above because we only purchase it to avoid personal liability for ridiculously priced emergency treatments and/or other costly procedures, if or when this might be required. I.e., *figuratively speaking... to avoid bankruptcy.*

And in the U.S., we can consult any medical practitioner, shop around for better drug prices, make online appointments for medical procedures, pay discounted cash prices for laboratory tests, receive immediate medical attention for most *anything*, negotiate discounts for cash payments to providers, and so on.

I am not suggesting that one system is better than the other. And I realize that my comments above represent a high-level summary.

Many people might offer counterarguments, including sharing their personal experiences, both good and bad.

But what I summarized above are basic facts.

Most people will surely agree that no person should face bankruptcy because of a sudden illness or health emergency. On the other hand, no person should have to wait more than a year for a hip- or knee replacement. Or elect to travel to another country - if they can afford to do so - for immediate medical attention. High profile, wealthy people, including Canadian politicians, travel to the Unites States frequently for this very reason.

And finally, on this topic, general practice physicians in Canada are government employees. They often say things like, "We are not taking new patients." Or they might work for two hours in the morning, take a 2-hour lunch break, and return for two more working hours in the afternoon.

There is no incentive for medical professionals to be productive because they are employed by the government, enjoy job security, annual union-negotiated wage increases, and extremely low-pressure work environments.

*****

Here is the good part about Canada: other than for the generally high cost of living (rent/mortgages, utilities, and food), the lifestyle is great, and most people are quite comfortable.

The latter is true, both psychologically and financially. For the most part, Canadians believe they live in the greatest country on earth. And financially, for as long as they are gainfully employed, enjoy a comfortable lifestyle.

One personal quirk about Canada's uniqueness is that the provincial governments own retail liquor stores. These stores are generally very beautifully appointed and well stocked. But because of the government-run monopoly, prices for alcoholic beverages are sky-high.

Most Canadians either do not care, or do not know any different. And after all, consumption of alcoholic beverages is voluntary. If you enjoy an occasional glass of wine, know that a bottle of wine purchased from an Ontario Liquor Control Board (LCBO) retail store, would be *the same* price as a few bottles of *the same* wine, purchased from a local Walmart store in the USA.

For example, a decent bottle of wine can cost less than US$10 at Costco in the United States. In Canada, the LCBO might sell that same bottle of wine for CAD$40. If we ignore the currency exchange rate for a minute, we immediately know that the government - as importer, distributor, and retailer - is generating a healthy margin from alcoholic beverage sales!

This too, is an example of a socialized system, with no allowance for competition.

High taxes are required to sustain government-managed systems. And that is before accounting for typical government overspending, inefficiency, general mismanagement, lack of productivity, and dysfunction. There are simply no employee rewards or incentives that encourage improved competitiveness!

In 2017, the Canadian Institute for Health Information reported that healthcare spending was $242 billion. This was about 12 percent of Canada's entire gross domestic product (GDP) for that year.

The World Health Organization lists Canada's per capita spending among the most expensive healthcare systems in the Organization for Economic Co-operation and Development (OECD).

*****

Like most other employable Canadians, I explored job opportunities.

Despite my tax-related misgivings shared above, I realized that earning an annual salary of $100,000 would put about $50,000 into my pocket, after income tax.

But it would be difficult to find a job with a salary that high. The average Canadian gross income - at the time - was less than $50,000 per person, annually

To generate $50,000 in personal earnings after tax from the sale of my photographic accessory products - which had already become a struggle due to the global shift from traditional 35mm film cameras to digital - I would have needed to generate about $150,000 in revenue.

And to generate that amount of revenue, I would need more storage and perhaps even employ people to assist. That would drive up my costs and then I would have to generate more revenue.

A vicious circle.

We had a decent amount of cash on hand, which helped to eliminate any desperation.

I pondered my options open-mindedly, wondering whether I should:

1. Open a retail business like my South African businesses from before, starting over.
2. Diversify into other, new, or more product categories.
3. Become a manufacturer's representative. This would allow me to focus on sales and business development while the manufacturer would be required to manage product storage, shipping, logistics, chase the receivables, etc.
4. Explore a personal adjustment from my typical 70-hour, self-employed workweek... take a step back, strive to become gainfully employed working 40

hours per week like a *normal* person... and learn to adapt to my new country in a different manner for a year or two, as a salaried employee.

*****

Ceridian.

After much consideration, taking a job was the path I elected to pursue.

It turned out great, in hindsight, because joining Ceridian created a path to my eventual introduction and affinity for Wall Street, stocks and bonds, equity investments, and more.

At the end of 2000, after living in Canada for two years, I joined Ceridian as a sales representative.

It was a humble position, given my experience. It offered an annual base salary matching the Canadian average annual income per person, mentioned earlier.

Ceridian offered great benefits. But most importantly, the company had an uncapped commission incentive plan for salespeople.

Did you miss the piece about my experience selling encyclopedias door to door?

I was convinced that if my Canadian peers could sell payroll and benefit services to large corporations, then so could I.

New sales representatives were afforded three months of paid, on-the-job training, without a sales quota to achieve.

But the ramp-up and learning curve would be steep. In a different tax jurisdiction (previously in South Africa) I had only ever signed the front of paychecks for my employees.

Unlike my peers, I had no knowledge of gross-to-net payroll tabulations, various employee deductions or allowances, and employment-related benefits.

Especially in Canada… I had never even seen a Canadian pay-stub!

*****

I had previously learned that trying to make a sale to the most difficult customer, would be most rewarding in the long run.

I thought to attack the problem of generating a decent list of qualified sales prospects by starting to call on corporations that had previously declined to do business with Ceridian, for what-ever reason.

In other words, my immediate sales prospect target list was my predecessor's client records tagged as *Sales Opportunity Declined* in our salesforce automation software tool.

I would be able to gain experience.

It seemed to be a low-risk strategy.

By adopting this method, I could learn without potentially muddying the water with a potential new sales prospect due to my lack of knowledge, limited understanding of our business (and theirs), not knowing the sales triggers that would prompt a buying decision, ignorance of the nuances related to this legacy business model, etc.

Within a few months - and after nearly quitting due to personal frustration at my inability to generate sales quickly - I started to figure it out. My peers were mostly selling payroll services, back-end processing of employee salaries, tax slips, etc.

I changed my focus and started offering solutions to business problems. I learned and began to understand North American compensation, as opposed to payroll.

I tried to figure out the drivers for a buying decision.

How was the person I was trying to sell to, personally compensated? What was motivating them to even have a conversation with me? In simple terms, "Why are we having this meeting?"

Sometimes, I would literally ask the prospective client this last question above.

In a way, I was fortunate.

I had a weird accent. I was not from Canada. I was therefore not necessarily expected to automatically understand their customs, processes, and methodologies. In a way, I had a built-in element of forgiveness, as an allowance for disrupting their status quo.

We had one major competitor, ADP.

Usually, larger clients would go to market and invite bids from competitors to show their shareholders and stakeholders that they had done their due diligence. This was often a charade.

They would typically issue a Request for a Proposal (RFP) just to show that they had invited competitive bids, and then renew with the incumbent vendor anyway.

I had to figure out these nuisance sales objections to be able to win.

My revenue target, once it kicked in, was $400,000 for one year. Exceeding this target would result in a near doubling of my base salary.

But to achieve the sales quota, I needed to create a pipeline of potential sales opportunities that would *move the needle* at a steady clip.

Generating e.g., $20,000-30,000 per month - the average sales contract order value per new client - would not cut it.

I would fall short of my target unless I added more than one new client per month. That would be a stretch goal. My team members were closing less than ten new deals per year, and they were falling short of their sales targets.

Achieving the target set before me required identifying and then successfully executing a sale with at least one *whale* that would push me over the edge, in terms of sales performance.

This became my baker's dozen sales funnel objective: at any time, I needed *12 smaller- + 1 whale-sized* corporate clients in my pipeline of qualified sales prospects.

I became the first sales representative in the corporate sales division to hit my sales quota in that first year. By the next year, I entered the full fiscal year already ramped-up. I had a qualified sales funnel that easily exceeded my sales quota. I just needed to execute and close deals.

The job became easier.

New businesses were starting. They were easy pickings.

Like chip manufacturers. Not potato chips, but computer chips. Well-funded, venture-backed startups with a hundred or more people on the payroll. I needed to get to them first.

I did.

I was learning to follow the money.

VC money, angel investors, and startup entrepreneurs in the news. And people who had compensation plans with stock options, restricted stock awards, performance shares... not just cash.

I had no idea what some of these things meant, never mind how they worked. But these topics were out there, in the news, and I knew a little more than most people. Enough to be dangerous!

But paying attention, and often faking my way through some of the conversations.

People asked me questions. Sometimes, I did not even know what they were asking me, let alone an answer to the question.

I learned to ask, often, "Walk me through how you do this today."

They would go into lengthy explanations about their current system, usually a manual process, and frequently something that they made up for themselves, because no-one else knew any better either.

I took notes. Asked lots of questions.

Over time, I would become an expert.

*****

When my peers were selling payroll, I had moved to selling managed services. There was no such thing. I made it up.

My sales pitch became, "What if you could focus on [chip manufacturing], and we take care of all your human resources requirements for you?"

"Managed Payroll Services" became "Managed Human Resources".

There were no such things either. But it made sense to me. The company would be able to concentrate on their core competency, and we would serve them while focusing on ours.

Nobody was commonly using words like *Business Process Outsourcing* (BPO) in our industry. Not at that time anyway.

My modus operandi morphed into... "The answer is yes, what was the question?"

My first large deal was a computer manufacturing company called Dell. You might be familiar with them?

I fished, they nibbled. We worked together to try and achieve a common goal.

Dell would sell computers. Ceridian would take care of the payroll-related administrivia.

My sales presentation, and cost analysis, included the people-related expenses of their payroll department.

Our typical, total, annual fee for traditional payroll services was about half the cost of one full-time employee, earning an average annual Canadian salary.

But Dell Canada was larger in size than an average client. They had three employees working in the payroll office.

A business unit with three employees represented a fixed overhead cost that would exceed $120,000 annually for base salaries. Additional costs included benefits, software user licenses, employee workspaces, paid vacations or leaves, reimbursements for company expenses, etc.

This fixed cost above became the foundation of my business case. Our bureau-style payroll services offering for a company that size would have been about $60,000 per year.

My new potential deal, if we were to *take over* the entire payroll function, and before any add-ons, was therefore already close to $200,000.

A compelling pitch would be for us to either (a) deliver the entire payroll function for a lower annual cost, or (b) deliver better, more modern services, more efficiently and expertly... for about the same amount of money.

As you may recall, my annual sales quota was $400,000.

I managed to sell Dell as a new Ceridian client. The deal value was nearly $200,000.

The deal would enable them to focus on their core competency, which was building and selling computers and peripherals, while we became their outsourced, expert payroll services provider.

A win-win!

I managed to close another dozen (or so) deals that were in my pipeline already for that same fiscal year. Those new clients - although I might have sold three in some months and none in other months - generated nearly $300,000 in additional sales revenue for the year.

Sales quota: $400,000

Contracted sales revenue: ~$500,000

The sales commissions were good.

Not great, but good.

After a full year and a few months working as a sales representative, Ceridian promoted me to Small Business Sales Manager.

This was almost a step backwards, albeit financially more rewarding in terms of a predictable, increased base salary.

Sales to small businesses were simple and relatively easy. I often accompanied my sales representatives to a first sales call with a new prospective client, with a contract already drawn up and ready for their signature.

Sometimes the client would be a little taken aback by the aggressive approach, especially in Canada.

But at other times they just signed it on the spot, and we closed the deal.

I preferred this more aggressive approach with smaller businesses, at least for these reasons:

(1) Salespeople are often able to deal directly with the owner(s) or decision-maker, instead of an influencer.
(2) Small businesses usually make decisions quickly.
(3) My salespeople would be able to close the deal, hand the new client off to our implementation team, and focus on chasing the next, new deal instead of having to go back to the same small business sales prospect, multiple times like peers who were hunting for larger corporate clients.

Another year later Ceridian promoted me to Corporate Sales Management.

I now had my previous boss' job. The guy who had originally hired me. He had left the company after inheriting a tidy lump sum that allowed him to reconsider working for a living.

My team's total sales quota was about $8,000,000.

But my earnings were no longer commensurate with the corporation's sales revenue ask.

This annoyed me.

I brought it to the attention of my manager during our casual conversations a couple of times. He felt the same about his compensation but needed his job. For this reason, he did not want to rock the boat.

Then Ceridian's executive team decided to roll out a matrix management structure. I was now going to be called the Managed Services Board Director.

We created these matrixed boards, overseeing certain operational areas. I was now responsible for business development for the Managed Services Board and - simultaneously – for the Corporate Business Solutions Board, as vice president of sales.

Suddenly, I had two jobs. Along with responsibility for a $15,000,000 total sales target, or quota.

I had new and additional account management and salespeople reporting to me.

My *people management* responsibilities and corporate P&L responsibility was now greater than what my previous, personal business interests in South Africa had been.

The mental fork in my career path, at that time, was that in South Africa I owned most of the equity in my business.

At Ceridian, I owned hardly any equity. The company offered very few and limited performance-based stock rewards during my tenure, and seldom granted employees stock options.

*****

In financial jargon, a stock option award is a derivative contract. It derives its future value from the performance of an underlying entity, in this instance, the company's publicly traded stock.

For the sake of simplifying the concept, stock options work like this:

1. ABC's stock is currently trading on the stock exchange at $10.00/share.
2. ABC grants certain stock awards to their employees under the rules of their compensation plan. This serves two primary purposes:
    a. Being an owner of the company is motivating for most employees, and
    b. The company can utilize that ownership to help retain great employees.
3. An employee is awarded 1,000 shares of ABC's stock, at a price of $12.00/share. This award will vest (be available) in two years. The price and vesting period also serve two

purposes:

    a. The employee is motivated to be productive, which will probably help ABC's stock price go up, and

    b. The employee is likely to stay with the company for that two-year period, at least waiting until the stock award vests.

4. After two years, ABC's stock might be trading at $5.00, and the award is underwater, or has no value. This is simply business risk, because the future performance of a company's publicly traded stock is unpredictable.

5. But after two years, ABC's stock might be trading at $20.00/share. The employee could now either:

    a. *Buy and Hold*: Buy the 1,000 shares at the predetermined purchase price of $12.00/share (the option delivery price), if they had saved enough money to be able to afford an outright purchase; or

    b. *Sell to Cover*: Sell only enough of the shares to pay for the 1,000 shares and any taxes due, and keep the remaining shares; or

    c. *Cash out*: Use the proceeds of the sale to pay for the entire cost of the stock option award plus taxes due and keep the change.

Contrary to popular belief, stock options should not be regarded as free money for one-percenters.

Many cash-starved startups have offered employees stock instead of cash. When they started out, they might not have been able to afford to offer employees cash compensation, because they were pre-sales, or not generating cash.

To attract and retain employees, they might have offered stock as compensation - commensurate with the employee's experience or position with the company - instead of a decent salary.

Some employees at successful startups became millionaires and even billionaires because of their stock-based compensation. Think Facebook or Google, for example. But Silicon Valley is littered with failed startups and people who worked for meager wages, only to never hit the proverbial jackpot.

These equity awards represent compensation grants (or awards) that are meant to help ensure the collective success of the business, or otherwise.

In my example above, the employee would have a compensation plan that offers $X in regular wages plus an annual award of 1,000 shares, creating an opportunity for the employee to purchase ABC's stock at a predetermined price, at a future date (the derived value).

*****

Working at Ceridian was a great job, but without any equity, as mentioned previously.

Ceridian paid employees in sales-related roles a monthly base salary plus commission - based on sales contracts executed for the previous month.

Non-sales employees were typically paid a base salary. Some earned quarterly or annual bonuses for their labor. Like many employees do.

An employee could purchase Ceridian's publicly traded equity via the New York Stock Exchange (NYSE), but the company did not motivate the employees to become owners.

It selectively offered a few employees stock awards (or grants, like stock options), or participation in a discounted stock savings plan (commonly called an Employee Stock Purchase Plan, or ESPP).

Ceridian was eventually acquired for US$5.3 billion by Thomas H. Lee Partners and Fidelity National Financial. As a result, at that time, Ceridian's common stock ceased trading on the NYSE.

I had learned that being an average employee was a terrible deal. Working as an employee makes it nearly impossible to build significant equity, never mind generational wealth. And when employees eventually exit their day jobs, they cannot sell those jobs as part of an exit strategy.

They just leave. Although, sometimes, they depart with a nice gift as thanks for their tenure, and past work effort.

More importantly, learning how the tax system worked - in almost every country - caused me to reconsider becoming an employee again, unless I could own equity in the employer's business.

The simplicity of this lesson can easily be described in two sentences:

- Employees earn money as a reward for their work... withholdings (e.g., taxes) are deducted and *the employee gets to keep whatever is left over* after the applicable withholdings have been deducted.
- Entrepreneurs earn money as a reward for their work... pay all their expenses (including themselves and some out-of-pocket personal expenses) and *pay taxes on whatever is left over* after they have paid for those expenses.

Can you spot the difference?

I quit my job at Ceridian in December 2005.

*****

Solium Capital.

This Calgary-based Canadian startup company was in the business of administering, servicing, and recordkeeping equity and/or executive compensation plans.

A publicly traded company would, for example, offer its senior managers company stock as part of an executive compensation plan. There are several reasons why companies would do this:

- Executives become part-owners of the company, meaning that their interests are better aligned.
- If the business performs well the stock price might increase. All shareholders and employees who own the company's equity would be rewarded as a result.
- Stock option (and similar) awards usually vest over a few years. This means that the executives would be more likely to stay for those few years to earn that stock-based compensation in the future. In other words, equity plans help with employee retention.

But these equity programs are complicated and not easy to administer.

Legislative filings required to keep compensation plans and executive insiders compliant are onerous, putting awardees at risk. Top executives have been fined or imprisoned for stock manipulation and/or fraud. In this regard, Solium offered executives a *stay out of jail card.*

During the early part of 2006 - while mostly minding my own business, literally - I received a call from a friend. An executive recruiter. He informed me of a job that might be of interest to me.

A small, publicly traded company in Calgary, Alberta was looking to recruit a Vice President of Market Development.

Whatever that meant, specifically?!

I reviewed the job posting. I also looked at the company's performance over the previous few years. It was easy to do an analysis of the company's fundamentals because it was publicly traded, offering public financials.

At the time, Solium had reported revenue of about $5,000,000 for the previous year (2005).

The revenue generated on a per employee or per client basis was poor, but it had been growing. Solium had about 40 employees. The company was barely profitable, based on Earnings Before Income Tax, Depreciation and Amortization ("EBITDA"). It generated a small operating profit.

Quite a neat little startup, right within my wheelhouse, skills, and interest areas.

The latter included sales, business development, technology, and finance, although not necessarily in that order.

The President & CEO had previously served the company in the role they were looking to fill. The company was growing.

Solium positioned itself as a *Software as a Service* (SaaS) company... it was anything but!

The reverse was true. Internally, the company was heavily engaged in servicing clients. It had a small, but overworked call center, account managers engaging with clients on a regular basis, management calling on clients to help extinguish fires that flared up continuously, and more, like most startups.

Software requiring customer Service might have been a more apt description.

But SrcS does not sound nearly as sexy as SaaS!

The management team resembled a motley crew of typical startup employees.

One member of the original tech team, who had collaborated on the original software code, was trying to create an entry and foothold into the US market for Solium.

He failed to secure any sales traction, but he managed to identify and secure several useful business contacts. Incredibly good, in fact, for the company's future benefit and growth in the USA a few years later.

The CEO - at that time - had previously worked as a trader for a commercial bank's energy investment division.

The guy overseeing customer service viewed himself as an evangelist and missionary, but he was working at Solium to earn a living. He later left to become a missionary in Africa, before returning to Canada again, a few years later.

The Chief Technology Officer had extraordinarily little formal or technical training related to writing code, but she knew the software system, its quirks, and deficiencies. The software, like most software programs, was a work in progress.

The VP of Finance was a gem. She had been with the company nearly since its inception. Astute, polite, smart, and diligent.

That was the team I met, when I flew from Toronto to Calgary for a job interview with the entire executive team in attendance, in early 2006.

*****

Solium hired me.

I joined as VP, Market Development in June 2006.

I had delayed my arrival date a little. We had a family vacation planned for a visit to Japan that had already been booked and paid for, just prior to my start date.

I was going to work in Toronto, carrying the bag for Solium, selling their software and services.

Because the company was based in Western Canada, most of the (few) publicly traded companies out west either already knew about Solium and/or were existing clients.

In Eastern Canada, Solium was relatively unknown. The previous management team, several years before, had successfully sold one large financial institution as a client. That would be my foundation to build upon. One large, marquee brand name corporation, as an existing client.

Our potential clients were public issuers. In more simple language, publicly traded companies.

Toronto has a stock exchange serving the country's domestic public issuers. That listing of issuers would be my prospective client list, as Solium's sales hunter for Eastern Canada.

We had a great sales guy out west, in Calgary, who was already familiar with the company, software offering, pricing and most of the stuff that happens at most companies *behind the curtain*, unbeknownst to clients. He became my go-to guy for personal educational purposes.

In Toronto, we had one other employee. A gent who successfully disguised his lack of in-depth knowledge about the software and market requirements with a booming radio-style voice, and an air of self-confidence that made him believable in almost any circumstance.

He became, at the start, my software demo guy.

These two guys above, plus the CEO, who had hired me were my troika of foot soldiers that I would rely on for support, education, and personal development in the role.

The CEO was a stand-up guy, a gentleman, thinker, and listener. I really liked him, and we forged a great working relationship.

I was calling on potential clients in Ontario and Quebec.

Cold-calling sales prospects at typically larger, publicly traded corporations was a challenge. It was tough to connect with decision makers. It would take time, and I lack patience as a virtue.

Quebec would prove incredibly tough. This predominantly Canadian French language province in Canada is generally not welcoming to English-speaking Canadians. But I was a little fortunate in that I was not Canadian by birth and spoke with a weird accent.

There were probably not too many South Africans visiting Quebec for business in those days, so my accent alone provided unique entertainment value.

Plus, they offered me some linguistic forgiveness. This same forgiveness was not readily afforded to English-speaking Canadians who had not taken time to learn the Quebecois dialect.

Inexcusable!

Quebecers struck me as very insular. They probably viewed themselves as a threatened minority in Canada, but I cannot be sure. Perhaps they still do?

They go about doing business in an old school manner, mostly patriarchal, often requiring seeing the *whites of the other person's eyes* before agreeing to do business. I would fit in, easily.

However, I realized that our business prospects would be even better if I were able to recruit a local sales leader in Quebec.

Ideally, a mature businessman.

As you can tell from what I am sharing, I do not aspire to be politically correct. Senior male managers and owners - representing large corporations in Quebec - wanted to do business with people just like them. Although I cannot be certain, I am confident that this might still be the case, today.

But this comment above is true of most people.

That is why one will find groups of *similar people* in pockets across all urban centers, anywhere.

There are many examples all around us. Little Havana near

Miami. Or an area called Chinatown in almost every major city in the world. People living within walking distance of a religious temple. Groups of people flocking to areas where others speak the same, native language they speak.

I needed a Quebecer.

So, I set about trying to hire a suitable candidate as a sales representative for Quebec and Eastern Canada. As it was, 100% of the candidates who applied for my posted job were male. Only a couple of candidates were youngish, say, younger than 40. This made my assignment easier.

I hired a man who would become Solium's face, eyes, and ears in Quebec.

Later, some of my peers in Calgary would ask me to fire him, because they thought he was not perfectly suited to the sales role I had hired him for.

Many people simply cannot see a *big picture*, despite their best attempts and/or desires.

The people calling for his dismissal were wrong. At the time of writing, he was still working for Solium. And for as long as he - or someone like him - represents the *boots on the ground* in Quebec, Solium will continue to do business, and win business, in that province.

Clients and sales prospects viewed him as *the boss* of Solium in Quebec.

And he is a great guy too!

I now had a small team.

One person out west, a Quebecer in the east, with me as the sales manager and bag-carrying sales hunter centrally, based in Toronto, Ontario.

It took us about 6 months to ramp up and to start selling, but we made merry!

*****

Solium offered stock options, or equity, and a small base salary. The commission at 10% on contracted sales orders was uncapped.

In my second year with Solium I earned a tidy 6-figure income for the year. My gross pay was nearly double the income of my peers, mainly due to sales commissions earned.

The above sounds great, and it was, but remember that the Canadian government helped themselves to more than half of that income earned.

And I had to apply a large chunk of the change to servicing our everyday debt, utilities, food, etc. At this time... debt was a mortgage on our rather large family home.

Like most other middle-class, working people, I had also been indoctrinated into believing in *The American Dream.*

The foundation for this aspirational dreamland was government and media propaganda poorly disguised as encouragement for people to keep buying things they were unable to afford, like fancy homes and cars.

Furthermore, homeownership - which, for clarity, I support as a previous homeless person - contradicts the principle of *freedom*, because living and working in one place, robs people of their *mobility*.

Homeownership should be clearly defined as a home we own for the purposes of shelter, lifestyle, and safety... rather than a primary status symbol used to impress people we do not know!

*****

I was a top earner for at least one year, but I was not working for the money. Rather, I was working for equity.

Whenever my stock options vested and were available for exercise, I would use my savings to purchase the equity, and own the vested shares outright.

I did not sell some of my awarded shares to pay for the option award and applicable taxes (sell-to-cover).

No, I would just buy the stock... and hold.

Go long and stay strong!

For as long as I was entrusted with the responsibility for driving Solium's revenue generation and business development, I would own the company's stock.

At times, when I had some spare cash awaiting investment, I purchased Solium's stock on the open market (or via my vested stock options) for less than $1/share.

During the financial crisis of 2008/9, Solium's publicly traded stock hit a low of around $0.40/share. For quite some time, my cost basis for Solium shares was less than a dollar, about $0.88.

During that time, I was bringing in many executed sales contracts. Some larger deals were valued at around $1,000,000. The sales commission was 10%. But I shared the commission with my sales team, who had worked with me to win the deals.

At times, I did not allocate myself any sales commission. Instead, I negotiated a stock award as compensation for my sales efforts.

I wanted the equity rather than the cash. People tend to spend cash but tend to keep their investments, including equity.

For example, I sold Nortel Networks as a client before they later went out of business, after the financial crisis of 2008/9.

Previously, Nortel had been a major, *blue-chip* Canadian issuer.

This deal was worth nearly a million Canadian dollars. But I negotiated and accepted only 25,000 Solium shares as a stock option award with a future vesting date, rather than taking cash compensation.

Those stock options were awarded at a strike price of $1.00 per share. The first tranche of the stock award vested after two years. I sold all the shares about 5 years later for nearly $8.00 per share.

If I had accepted the cash compensation, I might have been tempted to treat myself to something nice.

For the eventual cash exit I generated from the sale of that equity tranche, I was able to treat myself and my family to another foundational building block for generating future, generational wealth for my family.

And still, I did not spend the money. I squirreled it away into an investment account and re-invested the cash into other equities.

An introduction to long-term wealth management. Learned because of having been homeless, rather than from an Ivy-League school.

*****

In 2008 - during the financial crisis of that year and the next - I transferred from Toronto to New York City. Like many people who arrive to do business in NYC we settled into a residential neighborhood in New Jersey.

Debbie and I purchased a small, humble home in a leafy NJ town called Florham Park.

I was now going to set about conquering the US market, also tapping into the great connections and resources that my predecessor had created for us, as mentioned previously.

When all the *wirehouses*, brokerage firms and investment bankers ran away from large, publicly traded, financially troubled entities like General Motors, I ran towards them.

I would offer a helping hand during a time of crisis. They were experiencing financial turmoil, but still had to manage their executive equity programs that included stock awards for their executives.

This was during a global financial crisis.

General Motors was widely mocked and ridiculed. Institutional bankers called the company Government Motors. I identified and connected with the person who had responsibility for managing their US$3 billion IT budget, and eventually sold them our software services.

General Motors was the last, large *Fortune 100 Company* sales deal Solium would win in the United States for nearly a decade thereafter, because my time with the company was coming to an end.

During this time, Solium was flush with cash. We were able to start acquiring small US businesses, delivering services that were similar or complementary to ours.

We learned that inorganic growth - mergers, acquisitions, and joint ventures - were good substitutes for a lack of organic growth, i.e., direct sales.

For a few years, there were very few companies to sell our services to. Many had offered their employees stock options (and similar compensation award programs) that were underwater. These compensation awards basically had no value because of the decline in the stock prices of the issuers.

I spent most of my time building a sales funnel for the future, exploring new sales territories - like the UK and Europe - while hunting for potential acquisition targets or partner companies.

*****

Around 2012, two of the investors who had originally capitalized Solium decided to return to the business fulltime.

They created an awful management structure. They named it the *Office of the Managing Director*.

In addition to themselves, they included the then current CEO and the gentleman I had referred to earlier, who had been a member of the coding team that had written the original version of the company's flagship software.

All four of them effectively held positions of equal power or authority, save for one - the primary investor and largest stock owner - who was also the company's Board Chair.

They divvied up portfolios for themselves and I ended up reporting to one of the come-back kids. He called his portfolio *Delivery* (effectively Sales & Marketing).

He felt inspired to tell people he was an expert marketer whenever opportunities for self-promotion were on offer, and much to my amusement.

But he was a nice guy. I really liked him.

My own portfolio - at that time I was the Executive Vice President, Global Sales - was going to be eliminated.

They started hiring new sales managers and sales representatives in jurisdictions where my sales team and I had previously been responsible for generating organic growth.

Regrettably, this exercise was an epic failure. I watched from the sidelines, becoming increasingly disillusioned and at least a little frustrated.

I am confident that GM was the last major US public issuer that Solium added as a client. To be fair, they successfully added some neat, well known *corporate brand names* as clients after my departure, but not one of the standing and stature of General Motors.

Some new marquee brand name clients - like Google, added later - turned out to be a small division or entity owned by Google, rather than the public issuer itself, or the mother ship known as Alphabet.

People hired into senior positions by *The Managing Directors* were almost without exception, terrible hires. Not terrible people. Rather, people who were seemingly incapable of visioning and/or achieving sustained organic growth and success in their respective portfolios.

Some of these new hires came and went. A few left and returned, just to leave again. Some were demoted into less senior positions.

Solium had become a revolving door for recruiting industry veterans previously discarded by other, larger previous employers. Recycled executive leaders from large companies like eTrade, Fidelity, Merrill Lynch, etc. People who had previously represented marquee brands, as if their resume or Rolodex would automatically open new doors of opportunity for Solium.

It did not work... not as expected anyway.

Yet Solium was profitable, flush with cash, firing on all cylinders.

Our company had become a perfect acquisition target for a larger corporation. We were generating cash. We had no debt. In such circumstances, a buyer might be tempted to ignore the scorpions found under every rock one turned over or lifted.

In the meantime, another personal exit strategy loomed. But this time it would be much easier.

I had built up some personal wealth and liquidity by way of a few real estate deals, careful management of my Solium stock option awards and other direct equity investments. I had achieved some great winning stock trades, trading public securities via a few self-directed brokerage investment accounts.

In early 2014. I quit.

It was one of the toughest decisions of my professional career. This company that I had helped to build was no longer my home away from home.

People often say that employees do not leave the company they work for. They leave the people they no longer desire to work with. This, for the most part, is true.

*****

During my tenure with Solium, I had enjoyed opportunities to work in multiple countries. In addition to Canada and the United States, I was doing business with people in Mexico City, London in the United Kingdom, and several countries in Europe.

Solium's first, major, new client in the UK was global beer brewing powerhouse, SABMiller. My very first sales prospect in the UK had become Solium's first client in London!

I have nothing but fond memories and gratitude for almost seven of the nearly eight years of my professional career, and time, that I had dedicated to working for Solium Capital.

Today, I honestly still miss many of my ex-colleagues and peers, but not all. Some of my ex-colleagues might read this sentence in the future and wonder to themselves… "Is he talking about me?"

If you are now staring at this page, pondering that question, then you might very well have influenced or hastened my departure.

My job was no longer fulfilling, nor challenging. My previous business development contributions and management responsibilities, which had resulted in Solium achieving net, new organic growth previously only imagined when I joined the CAD $5 million revenue company in 2006, had all been eliminated or diluted.

Many of the people that I had really enjoyed working with either started leaving the company under its new management structure or were openly talking about departing in the future.

As is typical in situations of dramatic change, many of the people who were threatening to leave at the time, are still there today. Under duress perhaps, because they lacked another opportunity worth exploring, or due to fear related to change, or uncertainty.

*****

I thought to include a couple of examples of how professional, sophisticated business leaders should never behave.

At one stage, *the Managing Directors* interviewed and (later) hired a U.S. Sales Manager. They did so without mentioning the creation of this new sales management role to me. At the time, my official title was still Executive Vice President, Global Sales.

They met and interviewed a candidate for the sales management position mentioned above, in a small boardroom just a few dozen feet from where the incumbent EVP Global Sales (me) was seated at his desk, busily minding their business.

The new hire lasted about one year in that sales leadership role. His legacy included the departure of Solium's best salespeople, a disorganized sales management structure, and zero sales. Yes, literally zero net, new organic sales contracts executed…. for almost an entire year.

At one stage, a senior salesperson had asked the new manager to accompany her on a sales visit to a large client.

His response: "I was hired to manage the sales team, not do sales for you."

*****

During another exciting moment, one of *the Managing Directors* sent out a company-wide email blast.

The subject was "Rudi is going to London."

In the text he mentioned that I had agreed to transfer to London UK, to head up our proposed new UK-based office, which was correct.

Then, a short while later, he asked if I could first go to San Francisco for six months or so… and relocate to London afterwards. We had acquired a small San Francisco business unit from a local bank - a carveout - and Solium needed leadership on the ground to help integrate the acquired assets.

I agreed and relocated to San Francisco.

I had signed a 6-month lease for an apartment, located in downtown SOMA near Folsom & Third. The apartment was a short walk from our offices located on Market Street, also downtown.

At the time, San Francisco was a thriving, bustling, fun city, with much to see and do. Today, the city's downtown core offers a rare mix of extreme wealth and abject poverty.

Rich tech employees must often step over homeless humans, feces and other filth, drug paraphernalia and even worse, to arrive at their high-tech places of work. Places where they are treated to stock options, high salaries, free snacks, games rooms and other accoutrements that apparently represent success, in Silicon Valley.

After a few months I inquired about my future relocation.

Stay in San Francisco a while longer?

Relocate to London?

No-one offered any ideas or suggestions.

They almost seemed to be at a loss as to what to do with me. The small company's insular corporate culture and leadership had become cancerous, consuming itself.

One of the Managing Directors wanted the London gig for himself. But he was a weak manager at home, and his wife and family delayed his move for a long time.

Eventually, he shared that he would be going to London, not me.

And that was that… a conclusion to a confusing, directionless period entirely devoid of clear strategy. And a signal that I had reached the end of my executive sales career at Solium Capital.

In the words of the famous English writer and poet, William Wordsworth, I found myself asking, "Was it for this?"

I did not have another job to go to. I was not pursuing other opportunities.

People are normal. I am weird.

It was just time for me to move on.

To go away and do something else.

*****

Eventually in 2019, Solium was acquired by Morgan Stanley for around US$900 million. This was equal to about 10x Solium's annual revenue, which had been mostly stagnant for several years after my departure.

Multiples on revenue (or earnings) are simple valuation metrics for acquisition pricing purposes.

One might use these as a guideline to argue whether a buyer overpaid, or whether the acquisition price had been a fair reflection of the assets acquired. As is always the case, hindsight is 20/20.

But Morgan Stanley likely acquired Solium Capital for less obvious reasons. Here are just a few:

- Morgan Stanley's existing equity compensation administration and record-keeping business was struggling, itself largely stagnant.
- Solium offered a warm introduction to some smaller, privately owned companies. This would allow Morgan Stanley a proverbial leg-up for underwriting future IPOs.
- Morgan Stanley's wealth management division needed a boost, especially in a declining equity compensation market. The number of public issuers were declining year after year due to takeovers, mergers, and bankruptcies.
- In the same manner that Solium had elected to follow a path of inorganic growth in the United States due to a lack of new business origination, Morgan Stanley would be able to significantly increase their market share by way of this acquisition.

-         As smaller equity compensation companies were acquired or went out of business, this niche equity compensation product and/or service offering also declined with the broader market. This was exacerbated by the decreasing number of publicly traded companies, and lack of IPO activity. By acquiring Solium Capital, Morgan Stanley effectively reduced any competition in the marketplace to exceedingly small, localized vendors, transfer agents and banks offering record-keeping services, and a couple of wirehouses still offering similar services.

There are several reasons why this acquisition might not have been a great deal for Morgan Stanley. But, because I am delighted and impressed by this successful divestiture by my ex-colleagues, I will forego any negativity.

I am delighted that many of my friends became quite wealthy because of this acquisition. I am happy for their success and good fortune after many years of hard slog! I too had obviously benefited greatly from equity ownership in Solium shares when it was a publicly traded company.

The average cost basis of my Solium stock holding was around $1.00/share. The prices I achieved as I sold out of my stock positions represented a generous and favorable risk/reward ratio, in exchange for the time I had invested with the company.

Deferred compensation as a reward for having helped a small business grow into a slightly larger business!

*****

In February 2019 I wrote to James Gorman, CEO of Morgan Stanley.

I offered my assistance - if needed - to help integrate his recently acquired asset. I was familiar with the company, its people, products, and services, etc. In addition, I could also offer some value and insight into operational issues *behind the curtain* that would have taken their due diligence team a long time to uncover and repair, as/if required.

As was his wont, Mr. Gorman never responded.

This did not matter in the greater scheme of things. I had only offered my services because I had valuable skills, insider knowledge and bandwidth available. At the time, I was spending most of my time helping Debbie to oversee our family's charitable foundation.

But I would have been able to allocate a chunk of my time to Morgan Stanley, quite easily.

As had been my custom, I was marching to my own drum, literally and figuratively, and minding my own business.

I wish them all great future success!

*****

CHAPTER 9

SOCIAL IMPACT

Early in 2011, while I was working at Solium, my family and I started a charitable foundation.

We had been fortunate to achieve business success.

We had reached a stage in our lives where we realized that we were able to start giving back, *pay it forward*, make a social impact, or to make being charitable our everyday mission… whichever of these you might prefer.

*****

Our decision to focus on philanthropy was hastened by an unfortunate event.

Debbie and I were friends with a family who were our neighbors in Toronto, where we had lived until the summer of 2008.

In January 2011, their youngest son died unexpectedly, after a brief period of illness.

A few weeks prior to his death, at the age of 15, his parents had thought - based on a doctor's diagnosis - that his illness was a severe bout of influenza.

But the diagnosis suddenly changed. He had been suffering from a progressive form of juvenile leukemia.

My family and I were quite stunned by his untimely passing.

We explored the typical questions that people perhaps ponder when facing situations of grief or sadness:

What should we do? Send flowers? Send a card?

These actions, perhaps despite good intent, seemed rather meaningless.

Our son - who had been friends at school with the teenaged boy and his older brother - suggested we should plant a tree.

I thought that was a good idea. Then he challenged Debbie and I with a better proposition.

He asked, "Why only one tree?"

After some deliberation and discussion, including with the parents of the young man who had passed, my family and I founded Memory Trees Corporation in January 2011.

Founding Mission: "Giving Back Life… In Abundance".

We envisioned that Memory Trees would be a charitable foundation focused on funding, arranging, and managing the planting of memorial and commemorative trees.

We would deliver services to people who had lost loved ones, in memory of people who had delivered outstanding contributions for public good, war heroes who had admirably served their country and its peoples, etc.

*****

During the day I continued working at Solium. In the evenings and on weekends, I was working to complete an MBA program via a university in the UK.

Our younger son was in his senior year at high school.

Debbie started to invest most of her time focusing on our new charitable business venture. We assisted Debbie from time to time.

Every now and then, random people would inquire about memorial trees.

We listened, and tried our best to attend to requests and/or unique requirements. Generally, someone was motivated to do something *in memory* of a loved-one.

We filed for tax-exempt status under IRS Code 501(c)3, and the corporation became a registered charity in September that same year.

We had no idea how charities operated, generated funds, organized themselves, etc.

But sometimes, ignorance is bliss!

We went about our business with the mindset of "people who suggest that it cannot be done, should not get in the way of the people who are busy doing it".

We did not know that charities were able to write grant funding applications and requests. For the first few years we self-funded... much like any other private, charitable, family foundation.

*****

A few years later, we met a representative working on a project in Palm Beach County, Florida. The project - that had received funding for two years from an organization called the Robert Wood Johnson Foundation - was called Healthy Kids, Healthy Communities.

Their primary mission was to create healthy spaces for school children at local schools.

Typically, this meant that they would install an edible, production garden where kids would learn to plant, nurture, and eventually harvest fresh produce.

The local program management team was quite efficient at fundraising. Soon, the foundation's funding grant - as primary program sponsor - was dwarfed by additional, or matched funds, generated via donations received from other donors. These included foundations, nonprofits and even a large state agency.

The original foundation's grant was for about US$300,000. But the program managers successfully raised about $1.7 million for the project. This was an outstanding achievement!

I was learning about fundraising.

However, I did not like what I was learning.

I am confident that one does not need to be a master gardener, horticulturist, or agricultural expert to understand that $2 million represents an exorbitant amount of money for the relatively simple task of building a few, small school gardens.

To the credit of the program managers, they had also allocated some capital to a walking trail and made funds available for the purchase and installation of exercise equipment at an existing, public park.

But they built less than 30 school gardens.

Some expenses related to the implementation of various projects were borne by other organizations - i.e., additional project funds - or donated by businesses or nonprofits.

Memory Trees assisted the "Healthy Kids, Healthy Communities" project team with the construction of school gardens and planting of fruit orchards. At our own expense. Our contributions were either self-funded, or we raised funds from donors to purchase required materials and supplies.

We did not know any better!

The program managers did not offer to provide our small corporation with any funding to help support our expenses for labor, materials and/or supplies. Not even once.

One might argue that Memory Trees, as a charitable foundation, should be viewed as a contributor and not an expense to the project. I would accept that criticism. But at the same time, should our charitable foundation status preclude a program manager - with loads of cash on hand - from offering a financial contribution for our work?

I only learned about the $1.7 million funding they had raised for the project, after it had ended.

I read their report that included glowing references about Memory Trees and our participation in the program. And I read the report's program budget.

I reviewed their outcomes- and impact statements. A nature walk, exercise equipment, and less than 30 school gardens installed. I thought out loud, "even if we assumed an allocation of $700,000 for the nature trail and exercise equipment, we would still be left with $1 million for 30 school gardens."

The math just did not add up.

*****

I was learning about nonprofits. I did not like what I was learning.

Small, typically family run nonprofits, do great work on shoestring budgets, basically living hand to mouth.

As a rule, small nonprofits are non-governmental organizations (NGOs) with annual budgets below $2 million. Mid-sized NGOs might have a budget between $2-10 million.

An NGO that generates more than $10 million might be viewed as a small business in general financial terms. But, as a nonprofit entity whose funds should be allocated *for good* rather than *for profit*, generating revenue greater than $10 million, is a large amount of money.

This is especially true when that revenue is generated entirely from gifts, grants, and donations from well-meaning and kind donors... as opposed to revenue generated from sales of products and/or services.

Everyone has probably heard, or read about, large foundations like the Red Cross, or Clinton Foundation, that seem to exist primarily for the purpose of enriching its executive team, founders, or both.

Like global chapters of the Red Cross generating billions in funding for victims of the 2004 tsunami... and distributing millions.

Or the Clinton Foundation that generated about $9 billion for Haitian relief after the 2010 earthquake, and then funneled about $600 million to the Haitian government and other Haitian organizations.

These are facts that can easily be researched and verified in the public domain.

*****

"Who owns a nonprofit?"

The answer is... "no-one, and everyone".

A nonprofit corporation or charitable foundation does not have owners, i.e., people or entities that own the equity of that organization.

A tax-exempt organization is granted tax-exempt status by the federal government. It generally serves a targeted group of people, delivering services and/or performing work like a government entity. Usually non-governmental organizations (NGOs) step in where a government agency cannot do similar work itself, typically on a much smaller, localized level.

Using the example shared earlier, the federal government would be hard pressed to create and deliver a children's education and health-focused program like "Healthy Kids, Healthy Communities" in one county, in one state, in the United States of America.

Therefore, these NGO partnerships exist, and often flourish.

But my moral compass was spinning out of control.

*****

Another great example is one of America's favorite charities, the United Way.

With local chapters across the country, they offer employees of US corporations an easy way to make charitable donations, typically received by the United Way via employer payroll deductions.

To illustrate my point, we will take a brief look at a local United Way chapter.

Anyone can review a US-registered 501(c)3 organization's Form 990. This filing is their NGO's annual Statement of Activities (or Profit & Loss) and Statement of Financial Position (or Balance Sheet).

A Form 990 filing also describes a charitable corporation's programs, donations made, larger donations received, and more.

Here is a brief overview of a local United Way chapter's 990 for a recent financial reporting period:

-    Total revenue: about $17 million
-    Top donor: Publix Supermarkets: about $3.2 million
-    CEO compensation: about $270,000

Nothing is particularly striking about the information above.

And the local chapter of the United Way provides financial funding support for many deserving agencies, like a local Food Bank.

And the CEO's compensation in relation to the organization's annual revenue, as one benchmark, is arguably within an acceptable range for similar-sized organizations, even relatively low.

But there is a subtext to the information provided.

At the time of writing, the average employee wage at Publix Supermarkets was $12.03 per hour. These lower-paid employees contribute to the United Way via payroll deductions. Presumably, their ongoing donations provide a sense of giving, doing good, helping others who are perhaps less fortunate than themselves.

In the United States, like in many other countries, there is much discussion about the growing gap between the rich and the poor. But very few people - including those who complain the loudest - choose to acknowledge their personal contribution to this macro problem.

The Publix supermarket employees are contributing - first - to the executive and staff salaries of the United Way, before any contributions are allocated to charitable causes.

Also, at the time of writing, this United Way chapter employed a staff of about forty people.

At a relatively modest average salary, with benefits, a forty-person payroll represents an annual expense of around $2,000,000. In real terms, the $12/hour employees are first contributing to this payroll expense, before any donations, gifts and other contributions can be granted to nonprofit agencies.

Much like working for the government, working for an organization like the United Way or Red Cross offers job security, a decent salary, and reasonable benefits. Hardly anyone ever gets fired from nonprofit foundations, regardless of their individual levels of productivity and/or contributions, or lack thereof.

Similarly, at a federal level, ongoing payroll tax contributions of working people that are withheld and automatically deducted from employee wages, end up funding the rather lavish lifestyles of elected *leaders*.

A counterargument might be to say, "That is just how it works."

However, charitable donations - much like our personal taxes - should arguably first be allocated to cover the costs of programs for which the contributions were intended, and then, operational costs.

Ironically, when foundations - like the United Way - offer to fund another nonprofit organization's programs, they frequently insist that their funding support may not be used to fund the beneficiary's operational costs, including salaries. Or they will set some restriction, or limit (e.g. a percentage) to ensure that the grantee organization will not use the entire grant for overhead expenses.

These types of restrictions create an interesting conundrum. Many charitable organizations offer services, like healthcare, tax filings, etc. These are service-type NGOs. Their primary overhead is staff and human resource-related expenses. Their budget for materials and supplies, for example, might be $0.

Unless a funder agrees that their grant funding will be applied entirely, in the first place, to salary overhead, such a service-oriented NGO will not be able to function, despite their best intent.

In other words, the *do as I say and not as I do* rule is often activated before any charitable grants or allocations will be awarded.

Imagine - for a minute - an investor purchasing a large lot of shares in a publicly traded corporation, and then insisting on the way his or her invested cash should be spent, utilized, or allocated within (or by) that corporation. No sane business leader - unless totally financially desperate for example, as we had observed during the financial meltdown of 2008/9 - would accept such an offer.

To this end, my family and I also tried to shy away from accepting any funding for charitable programs that *have strings attached*.

For the most part, we would be fiercely independent.

*****

A well-compensated CEO of a publicly traded, blue chip corporation - like JP Morgan Chase or Walmart - will always attract attention for his or her large paycheck.

Whether their compensation is justified or not, is irrelevant to the point I am making.

People ignore the wealth gap problem on a micro level. It is easy to become distracted by the squeaky wheels that make the most noise.

So, when the United Way draws people's attention to the growing divide between the haves and the have-nots, they conveniently ignore the fact that their underworked, overpaid CEO makes more than 10x the average annual earnings of the Publix employees, who are paying that CEO's salary.

This transfer of wealth resembles a proverbial *daylight robbery*. The rich stealing from the poor, rather than the other way around.

The medieval feudal system was an institutionalized capture of wealth by the overlords.

Today, we call this *business as usual*.

Business we might well be personally engaged in, while pointing fingers at others.

Do as I say... and not as I do.

*****

Our charitable foundation was delivering several community revitalization and upliftment projects.

Since the time I had left Solium, Debbie had managed our program interaction and cooperation with "Healthy Kids, Healthy Communities". That project ended a couple of years later. I had enjoyed superficial involvement with our foundation and its charitable programs, only helping on occasion, as required.

Most of my time was spent trading stocks, which was becoming more of a vocation than a hobby. In fact, I was trading equities as if our lives depended on it, because the management of our equity investments represented our primary source of income.

But in 2016, I was ready to start contributing to some of our charitable work programs. Dividing my time between playing the stock market and working for Memory Trees, as a way of giving back to those less fortunate.

A personal charitable contribution, in addition to our cash contributions for the organization's operational expenses.

After all, the most valuable commodity anyone can offer is time, because it is finite.

Fresh from the project Debbie and our team had been working on, we had also undergone our first, significant evolution. We were now no longer focused on planting memorial and commemorative trees, but fruit trees and edible gardens.

After all, fruit trees deliver free food. The availability of this free food was subject only to where we had planted the fruit trees.

We were building community gardens, urban farms, and growing food.

It was time to forge some strategic partnerships, with like-minded organizations.

In 2016 the United Nations awarded Memory Trees Consultative Status with the U.N. Economic and Social Council ("ECOSOC").

In the politically divisive climate we live in today, I am no longer certain whether this status is beneficial, or detrimental to our organization.

Half of the American population would likely pat us on the back because of this high honor that had been bestowed upon our organization. Yet, the other half of the population might rather prefer to turn their backs on us for daring to be affiliated with the United Nations.

Association with the U.N. has become a subject about as divisive as the pro- and anti-Trump debate, with otherwise most typically placid people fueling the flames, spewing vitriol daily.

Our second strategic partnership was with our local State's Department of Economic Opportunity. They have a "Unique Abilities" program, focused on job skills and employment for people with various disabilities. For obvious reasons, this partnership seems less objectionable.

Growing food had become a primary occupation.

Debbie, our son, and I were now spending nearly all our time working - mostly without compensation - for our charitable foundation, figuring out how to solve the challenge posed by our new Mission: No Poverty, Zero Hunger and Good Health.

We were small, but mighty in terms of impact and outputs. Our organization's rather humble income statements belied our achievements.

Small, but mighty... was how one Community Foundation described us.

As the organization's treasurer, I had only ever recorded cash donations received from external donors, for financial reporting purposes, as required by legislation.

A nonprofit lawyer suggested that we should track and record all our in-kind contributions as well, because it would make the corporation seem much larger, in financial terms. This does not really matter to us, because our focus is dedicated to our work, rather than how people perceive us or the organization.

Memory Trees Corporation is really a private foundation, masquerading as a public charity.

The IRS defines a public charity as any nonprofit organization that generates more than one third of its revenue from external sources.

sΝΑΥ>RUDI BESTER

By their definition, that includes Memory Trees Corporation, because my family and I do not require, nor ask for tax donation receipts for funding that we provide to the organization.

And by way of my description above, I am not referring to the office space we donate, or our payment of capex and other overhead costs, etc. Those contributions are minimal when compared to our time, donated to the charity for the purposes of achieving our mission and vision.

As mentioned, time is the most precious commodity we have!

My philanthropic philosophy is quite simple:

If the elevator has taken you to the top floor... it is your duty to send it back down to pick up people who were left waiting on the ground floor.

*****

Strategically, we moved into a new direction.

Our community revitalization programs still included urban farming, but we added blight renewal. We started working with cities and counties to create programs that would uplift and revitalize areas of urban blight.

Our volunteers included some highly skilled resources, who were either unemployed or under-employed as new immigrants. We realized that our team of volunteers included an architect from Ecuador; an environmental engineer who had immigrated to the USA with her mother from Venezuela, an industrial engineer from the Dominican Republic, and a local student who was studying landscape architecture.

In some form or another, subject to their availability and family commitments, we hired them.

We now had a highly skilled team of professional people, none of whom were licensed to work in the United States, but working in their respective, skilled professional trades for Memory Trees. In a way, we resembled a general contracting firm, without being a licensed GC.

What it meant in practice, was that we were able to offer similar skills compared with any other environmental consulting firm, at an extremely competitive rate, or fee.

It also created a fork in the road for our charitable foundation because fees for services would become unrelated business income, and no longer tax-exempt.

To cure this defect, we created a for-profit entity to complement our charity. We simply called it Memory Trees LLC.

Our Memory Trees Companies - collectively - now delivered services to community associations, cities, Community Revitalization Agencies at local cities, government agencies, and more.

We allocated nearly 100% of our net profit generated by our for-profit business to our charity. These were either cash, or in-kind contributions, like rent forgiveness.

During this time, we started working with, and training young people with high functioning Autism. We offered opportunities for them to learn basic job skills, for example by learning landscaping work. And then we helped them to find paying jobs.

As our team of experts adapted to their new country, requalified, or graduated, we bid them farewell and took pride in the fact that we had been able to help new immigrants assimilate to their new, adopted country, while also helping them to achieve gainful employment.

At a macro level, we were helping to transform tax dependent people, into contributors.

None of what I am sharing represents a traditional charitable venture or business model. Nearly all nonprofits create and roll out a program, or multiple programs. Typically, they position themselves as an agency that provides a much-needed social service or products, like housing or food.

Nonprofit managers and their staff write grant requests, and any funds received via those grants - if awarded - often represent 100% of their revenue. Some nonprofits create fundraising events - like a fun run, or a charitable luncheon with a guest speaker - but these are often one-time revenue generators, and frequently run at a financial loss if poorly planned, organized, and executed.

In simple terms - especially in relation to smaller nonprofit agencies - no grant funding means no business, or worse... going out of business!

We resisted any ideas that would require our organization to be dependent on another organization for our survival.

We still build on that same foundation, today.

*****

During 2016 the United States was leading up to a very divisive presidential election, between Hillary Clinton and Donald Trump.

Personally, I questioned my willingness to remain in the United States. From time to time, I wondered out loud whether the political hatred and vitriol that was becoming increasingly more evident, would negatively impact the economy of the country.

Donald Trump did not cause the divisiveness. Rather, the divided peoples of the United States caused the rise of President Trump's eventual successful, but surprising election as the 45th President of the *Divided States of America*.

Whatever your opinion of the two candidates or their respective campaigns... Donald Trump probably represented the least offensive option of the two primary party candidates, and the voters could pick only one.

President Trump was smart enough to use the electoral college voting system to his advantage, comfortably winning 304 electoral votes (270 needed for victory).

Nearing the end of his first term, Democrat supporters of Ms. Clinton still reminded people - more than three years later - that she had won the "popular vote" by a huge margin.

Of course, the popular vote is largely irrelevant. It resembles the desperate cries of someone claiming victory in a race that no-one else was running.

The stock market seemed to have responded well to President Trump. In fact, he used and viewed the ever-increasing stock market boom as his personal scorecard. That is, until the novel coronavirus hit the US with a vengeance early in 2020, an election year and the last year of his first term.

President Trump managed to succeed in several other areas. Few people would likely argue that his job creation policies and reduced unemployment numbers were not impressive.

Of course, it would be impossible to guess what Clinton's successes or failures as president might have been.

We will never know.

*****

On December 22, 2017, the most sweeping tax legislation since the Tax Reform Act of 1986 was signed into law.

The Tax Cuts and Jobs Act of 2017 ("TCJA") made small reductions to income tax rates for most individual tax brackets, and significantly reduced the income tax rate for corporations.

But more importantly, from our point of view as a community and educational investment corporation, the TCJA included a new program, called Opportunity Zones.

The IRS website describes Opportunity Zones as follows:

> *"Qualified Opportunity Zones are designed to spur economic development and job creation in distressed communities by providing tax benefits to investors who invest eligible capital into these communities."*

And:

> *"Opportunity zones are an economic development tool - that is, they are designed to spur economic development and job creation in distressed communities."*

We identified a potential match between our charitable foundation's mission and focus areas, and the new investment opportunities created via designated Opportunity Zones.

We created an Opportunity Zone Fund, specifically for the purposes of allocating capital into distressed areas near our head office location in West Palm Beach, Florida.

Within a few miles of our office there were several designated opportunity zones.

I appointed myself as the Fund Manager for our Opportunity Zone Fund.

We would now spend a considerable amount of time reviewing, creating, and exploring investment opportunities and potential acquisitions in opportunity zones. The macro-objective was to inject capital into a distressed area, that would lead to job creation and blight renewal, over time.

Even though President Trump had hardly ever mentioned Opportunity Zones when he addressed the people, this program caused billions of investor dollars to be deployed into lower-income areas.

Wealthy people wanted to invest in Opportunity Zones to enjoy the deferred tax benefits. And of course, they also wanted their investments to generate a healthy return over the required investment period - typically ten years.

But, in the absence of designated opportunity zones, those investment billions might have been allocated elsewhere, or remained on the sidelines as cash awaiting investment.

The creation of Opportunity Zones was a legislative addition to the TCJA that drove job creation and community upliftment. Many people are unaware. This legislative action was a primary driver in many geographical areas for the Administration's overall claims of higher employment- and lower unemployment numbers.

Our Opportunity Zone Fund, MTC Equity Partners, made its first investment in February 2020. We acquired equity in a business located in an opportunity zone.

This business would deploy our investment capital to help spur growth and development, add inventory, create jobs, diversify into complementary products and services, and more.

The enactment of Opportunity Zone legislation, and the future expected, positive results of the program, provide a great example of something commonly referred to as "PPP" - Public, Private Partnerships.

Neither the government, nor private business, would be able to accomplish individually what they are able to achieve in partnership with one another, working collaboratively.

This might be an example of the adage, "If you can't beat them… join them."

RUDI BESTER

*****

PART TWO

"F.I.R.E."

FINANCIALLY INDEPENDENT

RETIRE EARLY

CHAPTER 10

HITS AND MISSES

By now, you might be thinking that my life to date has been perfect.

After all, who goes from being a homeless child to being retired from a professional business career at the relatively young age of 51?

And then being able to focus his or her time, full-time, to being charitable and helping others who are in need?

If you were able to view a highlights-reel of my life - especially prior to the existence of social media - you would be served a smorgasbord of personal failures along the way.

Thank goodness Facebook did not exist during my youth. I can only imagine what my generation would have been willing to share!

Here are just a few examples of significant life/business missteps:

- An inability to maintain an ongoing connection with my family and distant relatives, outside of my immediate family, that is, my spouse and two sons.

- Not successfully completing - at the time - a bachelor's degree program with a proposed accounting major, fully funded by a generous corporate benefactor.

- Multiple losses on the stock market, while going through a steep learning curve.

- A dozen or more failed startup business ventures in multiple countries.

- During my professional career I often unsuccessfully tried to find and/or create income-generating opportunities, earning no money as a result, for extended periods of time.

- Failure to protect business intellectual property and suffering a loss of intellectual capital and intangible assets... because business scavengers feasted on ignorance of victims, like me.

- and more

*****

Some of my biggest mistakes were mistakes of omission rather than commission.

These include things that were within my circle of competence, while I was busy sucking my thumb.

The omissions are the ones that hurt.

In early 1999, a trusted business partner and friend contacted me. His business - in Taiwan - had started to manufacture compact *memory sticks* for computers. These are commonly known as thumb, USB, flash, or jump drives, depending on where you are from.

He took time and demonstrated great patience while trying to educate me about the business opportunity, and the range of new products he was manufacturing.

He explained that it would be a game changer for people using computers, because they would be able to create portable, digital files. These, in turn, would be useful for saving data, sharing files, doing presentations, and so on.

If you are old enough to remember dial-up internet, you will likely also be able to understand where this conversation is going.

At the time, few people were sharing files via the internet. Nor were we working in shared drives or folders.

Heck, sometimes it took 5-10 minutes just to secure an internet connection. And that was only for checking email.

My friend explained the ease of use of his new product. He informed me that a person would be able to take a flash drive, insert it into a USB slot, and then save files or images to this compact, mobile storage device.

It all sounds simple, right?

But this technology was new. Most personal computers, in use at the time, did not even have a USB slot.

My friend said that he would like me to sell his flash drives into the North American market. I was living in Canada. To sweeten the deal, he offered me product exclusivity in Canada.

I was unable to wrap my head around this new product, its features, and the (now) obvious benefits. I too did not know what a USB slot was. This meant that I was trying to imagine everything, and how it all might work.

I simply neglected investing enough energy and time to learn!

In 2017, the worldwide flash memory market was worth about US$50 billion.

As personal consolation... I had not been presented with an opportunity to own *the market*.

But I had been offered a potential exclusive distribution arrangement in Canada and a general, but more competitive sales distribution opportunity in the huge and rapidly growing US home computing market.

Imagine capturing 0.1% of the entire global flash memory market after two decades.

Well, such a market slither - if successfully achieved - would have been worth about $50,000,000.

Sometimes it is our acts of omission rather than commission that negatively impact performance, results, achievement of personal goals or business objectives, wealth creation (or lack thereof), etc.

How will you spend your time?

After all, time is the most precious commodity we have!

*****

How about a highlights reel of people I have never met, but admire to some degree, albeit for different reasons?

Wayne Huizenga was an American businessman. He died recently, in 2018.

Mr. Huizenga was one of my business idols. I met one of his sons at a luncheon. We chatted for a few minutes.

Without specific reference to the Huizenga family, I will readily admit that I am significantly less impressed by people that inherit wealth, than people who had created that wealth in the first place.

Generational wealth!

Mr. Huizenga was the originator and mastermind behind two Fortune 500 companies, Waste Management and AutoNation.

Not one, but two!

Very few entrepreneurs will create even one.

As if that were not enough, along the way, Mr. Huizenga bought and expanded Blockbuster Video, waste disposal firm Republic Services, and lodging firm Extended Stay America.

*****

Like most successful entrepreneurs, he was not focused on one task. Nor did he strive to specialize in a single business discipline, like accounting, for example.

But not everyone is suited for self-employment or entrepreneurship. Some people are ideally suited to learning and practicing accounting and becoming a CPA, for example.

Many others have the perfect skillset to become specialists in a particular field, whether in accounting or medicine, carpentry, or masonry.

Entrepreneurs frequently lack the character traits that allow for single-minded, dedicated, and focused attention on one task, or job. They often appear somewhat scattered in approach, thought, or communication.

But the real reasons for their success include persistence, tenacity, and an ability to execute a plan, idea, or task!

We should not confuse self-employment - like a doctor or lawyer in private practice - with entrepreneurship.

An entrepreneur would seldom go to the same place or do the same thing every day.

By the way, single minded focus on one business discipline and/or its related areas of specialization, is admirable. I would even take this one step further... a willingness to work is admirable, period!

And all businesses need employees, complemented by various subject matter experts.

*****

The information shared above about Mr. Huizenga can easily be extrapolated to other superstar entrepreneurs.

Elon Musk has business interests that include building electric cars, installing solar panels, building hyperloops, and launching space missions to Mars. All forward-thinking, but not necessarily causally related, one with the other.

Richard Branson has businesses in media, transportation, telecommunications, etc.

A controversial example of a successful entrepreneur is ex-President Donald J. Trump.

Even if you disagree you might still consider Mr. Trump interesting, if nothing else. Now, before I lose half of my readers right here, please read this short thesis:

Mr. Trump had apparently inherited a (few) million dollars from his successful father. Many people inherit money, and squander it all away. But that is not relevant to the point I am making.

It is this: Mr. Trump - despite some arguably undesirable character traits and habits, and several failed business ventures along the way - built a successful real estate empire, became a leading reality, celebrity TV host, and eventually, against all odds... President of the United States of America.

Trump's successes mirror that of Arnold Schwarzenegger to some degree.

Born and raised in Austria, Mr. Schwarzenegger is somewhat challenged when required to communicate in English.

He was a successful bodybuilder who became an English-speaking actor and movie producer in America, and then (against all odds?) a Republican politician who served as 38th Governor of California from 2003 to 2011.

*****

I too have had many successes and failures along the way.

But unlike some of the people mentioned above, you would have been none the wiser if I had not elected to publicly share my story.

You would not have been aware of my existence.

Thomas Stanley and William Danko wrote a top-selling book, The Millionaire Next Door: The Surprising Secrets of America's Wealthy.

If you have not read this book, I suggest you do. It is entertaining and informative. As authors who are also academics, they share many examples of the habits and customs of typical millionaires next door.

Real world stuff.

Some of their research might surprise you. For me, on the other hand, they describe a lifestyle I am familiar with as a minimalist... to a degree, anyway.

Because it is such a relative concept, I am not sure how different people would define the concept of *being rich*.

For some people, *being rich* might mean that one can retire from the daily grind. Having saved and invested enough money to be able to forego a regular paycheck. Freedom from a daily routine, avoiding rush hour traffic, etc.?

For others, *being rich* may imply fulfilling a desire to travel from time to time, staying in nice hotels, and being waited on and served. Or having enough money to buy luxury goods, like a fancy new car, without having to worry too much about their bank balance.

Ironically, most of the people that I consider as *being rich* - including most of the people mentioned above - go to work every day.

But I would even use the term work loosely because that too is subject to interpretation.

For me, work is what I do, rather than where I might be.

Perhaps this example of mobility, personal freedom of choice and time self-management represents the first step on the ladder of freedom, in the context of defining *being rich*?

*****

My family and I own a downtown office suite which we use for our work. We call this our HQ. When we spend time at HQ we meet people, work on new philanthropic ideas and strategies, we debate and fine-tune our charitable projects, explore social impact investment initiatives, etc.

We have a light industrial unit, a warehouse with an office where we do different types of work, more product and manufacturing related.

The office area of our warehouse offers the same amenities as our downtown office suite. In other words, we could work equally comfortably from our office suite or our warehouse. This implies mobility and flexibility.

And we have a charitable, retail gift shop in Lake Worth, Florida. We also work there for several hours every week.

If we are not at one of our workplaces, we work from home.

In the four work environments described above we have the freedom to come and go, as we please.

We own the businesses.

We unlock and lock the doors when we go there to work.

But we work nearly every day. Work is an important activity and life philosophy for Debbie and me. If we were not working, what would we be doing instead?

Imagine being Elon Musk.

Musk probably has a home office. While he is at Tesla, he has an office or dedicated workspace there. The same would be true for SolarCity, Boring Company, or SpaceX, i.e., wherever he might find himself. And, when he travels for business purposes, his hotel room is a temporary office.

Update: Elon Musk acquired Twitter in April 2022, adding another worksite and responsibilities to his large portfolio.

We are not workaholics.

Rather, as mentioned previously, work is what we do, not where we are.

Our work does not define us... it is simply the daily activity that keeps our minds active, healthy, and busy!

*****

Most people probably aspire to going away on vacation from time to time.

People want to go somewhere nice, enjoy a change of scenery, experience different cultures, languages, cuisine, etc. Or they want to get away and go camping or sit at the beach and read a book... just to escape the daily grind!

When people who are not very wealthy take a vacation, they consume. In real terms, they will consume accommodation, food, entertainment, etc.

When wealthy people travel, they very often also invent or create, rather than being exclusively consumers of goods and/ or services. They might create content, like a YouTube video of their travels for others to consume.

Or they might double-dip by tacking a few days of personal downtime onto the end of a business trip. Those couple of extra days may constitute a perfect break that allows for visits to a historical site, wandering about in a museum, or even just relaxing at a sidewalk café to watch the locals pass by.

Wealthy people may visit the same, exotic location as a less wealthy person. But while wealthy people are there, they are exploring business opportunities. For example, they might be pondering the purchase of an inexpensive apartment near the beach that will generate future, passive rental income... until they decide to make a return visit.

While one person might be sitting on a deck chair reading a fictional novel, another person might be sitting on a nearby deck chair reading the local classified ads, or a real estate magazine that lists and offers local properties for sale.

I am not suggesting one practice is better, or preferred, versus the other.

Rather, I am only attempting to describe a different mindset. Debbie is particularly good at practicing this mindset, far more so than me.

Try this example for a rich vs. poor person's thought process, and mindset:

- A *less wealthy* person sees a canary yellow Bentley convertible, and desires to purchase or lease the car. They go to the Bentley dealer and inquire about the price. The car can be purchased for $300,000 or leased for $2,500/month. If they have savings of, for example, $500,000, they might be tempted to purchase this *liability*. Or, if they have a high-income job, they might be tempted to lease the car and incur a monthly liability of $2,500, plus the ongoing costs for insurance, maintenance, etc.

- A *wealthy* person desires to own and drive this same imaginary car, described above. She scans the market for a rental property that will produce ongoing income of about $2,500/month. A small multi-family rental unit might cost $300,000... the same price as the car. At full rental occupancy, this $300,000 investment will generate a cap rate of

10%, i.e., $30,000 per year. She acquires the property for the same amount as the sticker-price cost of the car. The $2,500/month income will cover the cost of the vehicle lease. In real terms, the cost for the vehicle did not change, but the wealthy person gets to drive the leased vehicle *for free*. Or, expressed differently, her passive income generated from tenants renting their homes, will pay for the lease of her vehicle. And she will own the income-generating property for as long as she would be willing to be a landlord, several leased, luxury vehicles later, should that be her desire.

Learn to think like a rich person!

*****

Once, Debbie and I watched Warren Buffet deliver a commencement speech at a university. Mr. Buffet, by the way, is the investment community's uber-cool grandpa!

During the speech Mr. Buffet shared something along these lines with the students:

> *You were fortunate to have been born in the greatest country, and greatest economy in the world. Anything I can do, you can do. We are mostly similar, except that you are younger than me. I can own a house, and you will be able to own a house. I have a car, and you will have a car. I can eat at McDonalds, and so can you. The only noticeable difference between me and you today, is when we travel.*

Think about this. Buffet lives in a modest home in Omaha. This is also a relatively modest location - not a big city teeming with people, businesses, and entertainment. He drives a modest car. He eats steak and fries at local restaurants, and regularly buys food at McDonalds. He spends his free time reading and playing bridge.

You can emulate everything immediately above.

"The difference is when we travel."

You might travel to an exotic destination on a commercial airline, and even squeeze into an inexpensive seat towards the rear of the plane. Comparatively, Mr. Buffet probably request his personal assistant to arrange his upcoming travel schedule with the pilot of his personal airplane.

You effectively can enjoy *the same life* as Warren Buffet, except perhaps, when you travel.

That is the only significant difference.

*****

Start by analyzing your monthly expenses.

For most people, their largest monthly/ongoing expenses include rent or mortgage payments (and related costs, like taxes, utilities, insurance, etc.), cars (and related costs; like insurance, gas, and maintenance), and food.

The needs above - excluding a car - are included in the pyramid of *basic needs* in the motivational theory in the psychology study of human need, known as Maslow's Hierarchy of Needs.

And all of these - including some form of transport - are reasonable in terms of being considered essential expenses. It is fair to expect that having a roof over one's head and food to eat are minimal, basic requirements for any human being. And having a car - or another type of personal transportation - is essential for most people to commute between work and home to earn a living.

If one were mortgage free, at least one major cost would be minimized (only utilities, insurance, property taxes, etc. remain).

This offers a lesson in money management.

- Wealthy people typically use debt - or leverage, because it sounds more sophisticated - to make money.
- People who are not wealthy typically use debt (like mortgages or car loans) to purchase things they cannot afford to buy. This is because they do not have enough liquidity and/or money saved up to pay cash for their purchase.

In my example of the canary yellow Bentley above, I mentioned the cost of the vehicle vs. the cost of a small, multi-family dwelling.

I assumed both at $300,000. This might not be correct, or a fair comparison.

Maybe the car costs more than that. Or we can assume that it would not be possible to buy a small, multi-family apartment for investment in New York City for $300,000.

But that was not my point. The point I was making was the philosophical difference between the mindset of a wealthy person compared with the mindset of a less wealthy person.

The additional, and related point is this: wealthy people typically live within their means. In fact, most of my wealthy friends - I have a few - spend far less money than they generate, on an ongoing basis.

You might offer a counter argument to the comment above. For example, you might want to suggest that rich people spend less than their income because their incomes are astronomically large. That would be true for a few people, like Bill Gates or Warren Buffet.

It would be tough to spend earnings of a few million dollars, every day.

Most wealthy people do not live within their means because their earnings (or means) are off the charts. Expressed differently, wealthy people do not spend less than what they earn because they earn incredibly high salaries. That thinking would be incorrect.

The stories about how the wealthy spend their money, are concepts I enjoyed reading about in the book mentioned above, *The Millionaire Next Door*.

Debbie and I live comfortably, in a small community of townhouses and villas (rowhouses with no one living above or below).

Our villa has two bedrooms and bathrooms, and an open-style kitchen, living and dining area. The total floorplan or footprint is about 1,200 sf. (approx. 120 square meters). We are empty nesters. The apartment layout and size are more than adequate for our needs.

Our total residential costs include condo dues, property taxes and utilities. Occasionally, we have some maintenance or repair costs. Added together, all the aforesaid adds up to just a few hundred dollars per month.

Like most relatively wealthy people, we are minimalists.

We have one car, a Ford Escape, also owned free and clear.

We do not have any debt.

Add our monthly food bill to the property bills described above, and the costs for running our little vehicle... and you end up with ongoing expenses of only just over $1,000 per month.

It would be fair to assume $1,500/month, which would of course require an after-tax annual income of $18,000.

But we will also include reasonable, yet generous discretionary spending of $1,000 per month in our personal budget. This additional $12,000 annual expenditure represents a figurative set-aside for travel, restaurants and entertainment, visits to- and gifts for our grandchildren, etc.

So now, without any income earned from labor, I look to achieve passive income (e.g., from investments) that can generate at least $30,000 per year, after tax.

Because the tax rate is outside of my control, I will add $20,000 in taxes to the above. We now need to earn $50,000 annually before tax, to support our relatively simple and humble lifestyle.

If $50,000 represents a 5% pre-tax return on investment, then I would need $1,000,000 invested to return $50,000 annually. That is a relatively easy calculation, right?

Doing the math, if I were able to achieve a 10% return on investment, I would only need to have $500,000 of assets under management, and so on.

Many employees rely on an annual increase in their salary to help them keep up with the cost of living. Some employees do not receive any cost-of-living adjustments (COLA) per year, and elect to find another job, at a higher pay.

Government employees sometimes enjoy a COLA of 6% annually, which compounds quite quickly. That is why, after a couple of decades of working for the government, a *lifer* might be earning a salary they would never be able to earn outside of government.

Of course, it is easy to offer someone a relatively high level of compensation when using other people's money to pay the bill. Regrettably - or fortunately - we are not the government.

Returning to the math above. I realize that I need either (1) a return on investment greater than 10% or (2) more invested capital to generate the $50,000 I require for my annual cost of living.

Here is the good news. The Dow (as in, the familiar index of 30 large, blue-chip US whales), has historically returned nearly 7% annually, for more than 100 years. This is true, despite recessions, depressions, corrections, sell-offs, presidential elections, wars, pandemics, etc.

In March 2020 - the start of the coronavirus pandemic stock market crash - the Dow lost more than 30% in just a few weeks. This implies that one third of the market valuation of the top 30 companies in the United States was wiped out, at least on paper, in just a few weeks.

Yet, a few months after hitting that recessionary market low, the same index regained more than 30%... meaning it had recovered about half the paper losses in just a few weeks.

I am therefore suggesting that if one were to adopt the Warren Buffet investment thesis - *buy and hold forever* - it would be possible, on average, to generate 6-7% annually by just investing in the Dow.

However, most of the Dow component stocks also pay quarterly dividends to their investors.

Some companies pay a relatively small dividend. Others much more. At the time of writing, Exxon offered an annual dividend yield of nearly 7%, while Visa offered its investors less than 1%.

If an investor had created a small index of three stocks - e.g., Exxon + IBM + Boeing - in April 2020, the annual dividend would be greater than 5%. Add that to the average Dow return referenced above, and you end up with a 12% annual return on investment.

If I needed to generate $50,000 from my investments, and my equities generated a 12% return annually, I would now only require about $400,000 in invested savings.

See where this is going?

In "Chapter 22: Mutual Funds, Epic Fail" I mentioned the high cost of investing in mutual funds. I do not want high costs eating into my return on investment because then I would be required to put more money at risk.

Therefore, I prefer owning equities to funds, like mutual funds, or even ETFs.

There is no cost attached to owning a stock of a company, except for the initial, minimal brokerage fee that might be charged once, at the time of trade execution. After buying the equity, you own it at no cost until you sell it, hopefully for a profit.

*****

Single stock risk is a concern for most investors.

And if it is not, it should be.

If you invest in a company's stock, you need to understand that you could lose all your money.

Large corporations have gone bankrupt before for various reasons (think Enron, or Nortel), while others have been reduced to a mere shadow of its former self (think Blackberry, or SEARS).

Nobody wants to make an investment and end up losing all your money!

There are many ways to avoid this. There are index funds (ETFs, not mutual funds), that mimic the market at an exceptionally low cost. In fact, almost zero.

Examples are plenty, but one could *purchase the entire Dow index* by investing in DIA. Their management fee is only 0.16% (as of April 2020).

Buying this index ETF mitigates the risk of owning single stocks. For example, if Chevron filed for bankruptcy, that would only represent one Dow component out of 30 stocks in the index. Presumably, the others would survive.

Also, at the time of writing, SPY offered an expense ratio of 0.09%, *virtually free of charge*.

SPY is one of the largest ETFs in the world, offering exposure to one of the most well-known equity investment benchmarks. SPY appeals to investors seeking to build a long-term portfolio that includes large cap U.S. stocks.

In addition to including a few Dow components, SPY also includes stocks like Facebook, Amazon, Berkshire Hathaway, and other blue-chip equities.

However, if an investor elected to invest in SPY, one would exchange the annual dividend of say Exxon - currently at 7% - for a more reasonable 2.3%.

On the other hand, an investor might be able to offset the lower anticipated annual dividend with a much greater annual SPY return on investment and share price growth than, for example, the stodgy old Dow stocks.

*****

CHAPTER 11

A FINANCIALLY SELF-SUFFICIENT PERSON'S TRIP DOWN FRUGALITY HIGHWAY

Just for fun, I thought to capture a highlights reel of typical behavioral traits of an unassuming millionaire, who might be living next door to you.

Some people label themselves as FIRE: Financially Independent, Retire Early. This chapter looks at how some FIRE afficionados would go about their daily lives.

But, for the sake of quick and ready examples, I will use traits and habits of FIRE-ready people, as adopted by Debbie and me.

Groceries and Shopping

Caviar and champagne?

This is what the rich eat and drink, right? Well, that may be what rich people do, but probably not every day.

How about a minimalist next door?

One of my own favorite light meals is a banana.

Or a slice of whole wheat bread with peanut butter. And sometimes, with honey.

Occasionally I go completely *lifestyles of the rich and famous* and add sliced banana to my slice of whole wheat bread with peanut butter, and honey!

Altogether, at once... savage!

Debbie's favorite food is protein, and mostly simple proteins. She likes her eggs poached, a variety of meats (including cured), various cheeses, and yoghurt.

Did you know you can poach a raw egg in a small bowl of tap water in under two minutes, in the microwave?

Drinks. We enjoy espresso, water, and coffee. We both enjoy a cold beer occasionally. Usually, a domestic beer for Debbie like Budweiser Light. I also drink Bud Light sometimes, but I prefer European beers like Heineken, or Stella.

We both enjoy red wine.

I hardly ever spend more than $10 per bottle, and mostly buy wine at Costco. Sometimes, you can pick up a carton (12) of reasonably good red wine at Costco for under $100.

After all, if the wine was good enough for Costco's buyer to purchase in large, container load quantities... then it surely is good enough also for me to purchase by the case, in dozens, or singles!

And I mean *we* shop ...as opposed to sending people to do our shopping for us.

And yes, we even shop at Walmart.

Gasp!

Not occasionally, but regularly. And at Publix, a local, smaller (than Walmart), privately owned supermarket chain. We hardly ever shop at fancy stores like Wholefoods.

In fact, we hardly ever shop for anything other than groceries because we do not really need anything.

There are a few sound reasons for us to support Walmart.

The target beneficiaries for our family's charitable foundation regularly shop at Walmart. This means we pay the same price for a loaf of bread or a gallon of milk, as they do. But it is even more important for us to know what the going prices are for the staple foods they purchase on a regular basis, for their families.

From time to time, we have owned Walmart stock.

That is another reason for us to support Walmart. As shareholders, we want the corporation to be successful. As if our personal financial wellbeing depends on it. Because in some small way it would, if you owned Walmart stock.

Small, because our diversified portfolio of blue-chip longs sometimes includes Walmart stock. If I were invested in Target, for example, I would default to shopping at Target.

It makes financial sense to support a company that you own. This is true even if your ownership stake in the corporation represents a fraction of one percent of the issuer's total quantity of outstanding common shares available for investors to trade, via the stock exchange.

However, we do have shopping habits that are probably different to yours.

During an overseas trip that included spending some time in Munich Germany, Debbie and I needed to purchase some personal toiletry products.

We went into a drugstore at the airport and bought whatever we needed.

Now... probably unlike your current, preferred brand of under-arm deodorant, we accidentally found a product that worked. As in, a deodorant that worked for nearly an entire day.

Since that introduction to a product we found by chance, we have been importing deodorant for the last six years or so.

I realize that this might sound somewhat pretentious. But in real terms the product is readily available, and we can purchase it online via Amazon Germany. Each unit costs less than €1.00. Shipping nearly doubles the price. The more one buys, the less expensive the shipping would be on a prorated basis.

For the sake of illustration, we can just price it at below €2.00 each including sales taxes and shipping.

This price is not vastly different from the price you might be paying for deodorant locally, that might not even offer the same efficacy.

The difference is when we travel.

When we travel, we also spend time sourcing products, ideas, items. We seek to learn about new services that people might purchase or consume. This inquisitiveness and related thinking, as I had mentioned before, is one of Debbie's core skills.

We explore business opportunities. Always.

Dining out

Yes, quite a lot!

After all, we are two mature, empty nesters.

Sometimes we go to nice places. Usually, we reserve going to nice restaurants when we travel.

When we travel, we are prepared to spend more generously.

If we had elected to go somewhere adventurous and/or exotic... we feel we might just as well treat ourselves to relatively luxurious hotel accommodation. And like most people, we will obviously spend more on food and drink, compared with when we are home.

But most of the time, at home, we will support local mom & pop-style restaurants.

The types of places where you can go for dinner wearing casual clothes, and where one is unlikely to require a reservation.

Also, we frequent places where people look, behave and dress mostly like us. Generally, when one is among likeminded people, they are unlikely to be judgmental. They do not stare when you order a beer, and perhaps another, because they are enjoying a beer as well.

Once, Debbie and I arrived at a supper club - which was also a highly rated steakhouse - for a late dinner date, in a big city. We arrived for dinner at 8 PM.

When we arrived at the door, it was locked. I knocked. A man opened the door and asked if he could assist. I replied, saying that the club had been recommended by a friend as a great steakhouse we should visit. We were hoping that the restaurant was open for dinner.

He smiled and thanked me for the compliment. He said they only open for business at 10 PM every evening.

The above is an example of what I mean when I refer to people who look, behave and dress like we do.

We are quite certain that the crowd arriving at around 10 PM would be much younger, louder, and certainly hipper and more fashionable than us.

*****

Another time, we went to a small restaurant, located on the outskirts of a large city. We had been there nearly twenty years prior.

La Perla's specialty was fresh lobsters. Locally, it was an exceedingly popular restaurant. It probably still is, but we have not been back in ten years since our last visit.

It is in Sea Point, near the most southern tip of South Africa. Thus, we are unable to get to La Perla frequently for some fresh lobster.

At the time we visited, it was 3 PM on a weekday afternoon.

The proprietor came to the table and asked us what we would like to drink, and whether we would like to see the menu.

We ordered some wine, and simply said, "We would like some fresh lobster".

A little while later, a server returned to the table with some freshly baked (or warm anyway) bread, and a large bowl with a house salad. Then he went back to the kitchen and returned with some plates and flatware, and another bowl filled with lobster tails.

That was lunch.

We left at 5 PM, before the regular dinner guests started arriving for pre-dinner drinks.

Our mid-afternoon lunch was expensive and a treat to remember, but without any fancy trappings. No starters. No desserts.

A great combination of protein, salad, bread, a glass of wine, and some ice water.

*****

We usually dine at family restaurants when we go out for lunch or dinner. Places where one can usually walk in without a reservation and find an open spot somewhere.

We often squeeze into a couple of chairs at the bar.

Between the locals. Blending in.

We typically do not need a table.

Just two chairs, and a bit of space at the bar.

Simple.

That is how we like it.

Clothes

We do have nice things.

In fact, we both have a few pieces of designer-brand clothing items purchased at Ross, or Marshalls. People in the U.S. will recognize these retail brand names.

These are stores where good quality, end of line, and discontinued goods go for their grand finale... a final attempt to become merchandise that will be sold and legally owned by thrifty shoppers.

Most of what we own was bought off the rack. We hardly ever require alterations.

Debbie also likes discount retail clothing stores like H&M and Forever 21. I buy clothes occasionally, as needed, at stores like the ones mentioned above.

Neither of us likes to purchase overpriced stuff, and we do not show off manufacturer's branding without receiving compensation in return.

For this reason, specifically, you will never see us wearing clothing like Nike, that has a manufacturer's brand name, logo, or service mark on the outside.

I am not a professional athlete.

Advertising Nike's clothing is a win for Nike. It offers me no upside. Rather, it offers me the obvious downside of having overpaid for an item of clothing that is the same as any other manufacturer's product, sans visible logo.

Travel

We travel for business, pleasure, or family purposes, probably more than most people.

One reason why we travel a lot is for business. Our charitable foundation is in consultative status with the U.N. Economic and Social Council ("ECOSOC"). The United Nations head office is in New York, and we live in southern Florida. We can only commute by airplane to get there within reasonable time.

Our older son and his family live in Toronto, Canada. So, we go there a few times a year.

We do not travel in style. Instead, we travel efficiently and economically.

The actual travel - for example flying on an airplane, and especially when one has done it many times before - is not the most exciting part of a new adventure or a visit to some far-away, interesting place.

We fly commercial. We are both relatively small in stature, and therefore fit into economy-sized seating with reasonable comfort. We do purchase upgrades for extra legroom from time to time. We do not purchase business or first-class tickets for the *free* meals or drinks.

The purpose behind the journey in the sky is only useful if it gets us to our destination in reasonable comfort, as fast as possible, and safely. In other words, we want to get the travel part out of the way in the most cost-efficient manner possible.

Once we have arrived at our destination, our spending habits change.

Quite dramatically.

We hardly ever stay with people we know, or family.

We prefer to rent a hotel room. Generally, a really nice hotel room. When you stay at a hotel, you are also inclined to eat in restaurants.

You might need to rent a car, depending on where you are, or need to go. These are standard additional travel costs for us.

*****

In 2019 - before the 2020 pandemic ended freedom of travel mobility for most people - we visited several countries, including Canada, to visit our son and his family.

But, for personal pleasure and to celebrate our wedding anniversary we took a trip to The Netherlands.

Debbie and I have a favorite band.

Epica, a Dutch band.

Their rock-opera-style music is unique, and not to everyone's taste. Epica serves up a combination of an exquisite female operatic lead vocal accompanied by heavy rock music backing, some male growl, and general head-banging-metal.

They were scheduled to perform in an open-air amphitheater in a small Dutch village, called Hertme.

Ironically, their performance date was scheduled for a Saturday evening, on the date of our wedding anniversary.

We flew from Ft. Lauderdale to New York. There, we had a short layover in an airport lounge before departing for London later that evening.

A pre-booked limo service picked us up at Heathrow Airport. We transferred to St Pancras International Station for a trip to Brussels, on the EuroStar high-speed train.

En route to Hertme, we stayed over in Brussels, Antwerp and then Rotterdam, commuting by train between these cities.

In Rotterdam, we picked up a rental car at the airport and drove to Hertme, a little town located about 2 hours east of Amsterdam.

We leisurely explored the area around Hertme, and then went to see Epica performing on the evening of our anniversary.

Later, we dropped off the rental car at Schiphol Airport just outside of Amsterdam. We hopped into an airport-city train to get to the Central Station in Amsterdam.

We spent many hours at the Van Gogh Museum and Rijksmuseum, respectively.

We did a couple of typical touristy things, for example, visiting the Tulip Museum and sampling beer at the Heineken factory. We also enjoyed sampling and tasting Dutch and Indonesian cuisine, and excellent coffees.

A few days later, we reversed the route mentioned above to make our way back home.

The expenses above were budgeted for in detail. Most of the travel and related costs were booked and paid for in advance, prior to our arrival. In other words, we knew exactly what the vacation would cost, even prior to our arrival at the local airport.

The budgeted, prepaid expenses included our Epica concert tickets, air travel, airport limo pickup, Eurostar rail tickets, all hotel bookings, museum tickets, and car rental.

Once there, we used a daily vacation budget allowance to pay for meals, gas, local rail tickets, entertainment, additional museum tickets, etc.

Our budget included a miscellaneous line for spur-of-the-moment purchases, or an unforeseen expense.

We considered the possibility of a large, unexpected expense. Our backup plan was ensuring we each carried a credit card with a matching PIN... required when paying by credit card in the European Union.

Unlike my example of Warren Buffet's private travel mentioned earlier, my itinerary represents a sum of parts, all 100% commercial.

In the true spirit of FIRE, we budgeted for everything upfront, leaving little to chance. Budgeting is a basic money management strategy that anyone can copy, and highly recommended.

Think like a wealthy person!

Fitness

Healthy body, healthy mind!

You have probably heard people say this.

Debbie and I exercise every day.

Well, almost every day. Sometimes, when it is raining quite heavily, we will take a day off. Or when we travel, we might miss a day or two of rigorous exercise. But we make up for that by walking a lot.

We usually go for a jog every morning, between 4-5 miles daily. Just a leisurely jog.

After all, we are both in our fifties!

If you find some form of exercise enjoyable and do it often, then you end up doing it routinely, without having to motivate yourself to get going.

It is even better if you have someone to do it with.

If you have an exercise partner, one person motivates the other. For example, once we get up in the morning, one of us will start putting on our exercise gear. This way, the slower one will just copy and get ready.

It becomes an unspoken ritual.

The only time we discuss going for a jog, is when we wake up to a heavy downpour. Even then, we might go for a jog later that same day or do a light workout on our home gym.

Many of our friends say they hate running. Or they have a medical-type excuse, like *bad knees*. But even some of these friends still go for a walk or a bike ride. Most of them are in reasonable shape for their age, like we are.

*****

But your diet is more important than your exercise routine.

Diet is not something you do from time to time, but rather something you do daily, a lifestyle.

Debbie and I know of two lovely *young* ladies. One recently celebrated her 100th birthday, and the other unfortunately died recently at the age of about 94.

Interesting case studies, for *the same* reason. They both followed a daily diet, 100% meat and potatoes.

They did not know one another. One still currently lives in Vancouver Canada, and the other - the lady who recently died - lived in Greenville SC.

The Vancouverite's grandson is a close friend. He - seemingly like his grandmother - maintains that the only *green food* worth eating is avocado.

I am not suggesting that people should not eat vegetables. I am sharing a story about two people who lived for more than 90 years each, who only ate meat and potatoes.

If you like to eat vegetables, you can still have some food now and then.

In fact, and to be fair, I love eating fruit.

Earlier on I shared that a banana is a favorite light meal. Sometimes this is also a light breakfast, along with a glass of milk.

On a typical day I usually enjoy 3-5 portions of fruit at lunchtime, in addition to my breakfast banana. Potatoes, meat, and small portions of rice round out my everyday diet.

This combination of daily exercise plus a reasonably healthy diet works to keep me in shape, and generally healthy.

I avoid taking drugs and try to avoid doctors and hospitals. This is especially fitting when one is living in the United States, where healthcare practitioners are often better salespeople than medical experts.

And anyway, not all people who visit doctors and hospitals end up being cured or getting better.

Large pharmaceutical companies generate billions of dollars in sales that, in turn, deliver *healthy* profits and quarterly dividends for shareholders.

It is better to invest in a pharmaceutical company than to be a consumer of their products.

Remember, for drug companies, the revenue and profits are in the maintenance prescriptions, not the cure.

If they can hook you onto their medicine for the rest of your life, they have won… and you have lost! Millions of people rely on prescription medications taken daily.

At the risk of offending, I am suggesting that using Lipitor to manage your cholesterol is not the same as using insulin to manage your blood sugar.

The aforesaid - albeit with some exceptions - is something you can control. At least to a degree. The latter might be genetic.

You probably know what I am referring to: sedentary, unhealthy lifestyle choices.

From the car to the office to the sofa and then to bed… and then we reverse this sequence daily.

And old-world habits. Like smoking whatever, including cigarettes, and drinking alcohol until you feel tipsy, or get a buzz.

Really?

Do people still do this?

If you cannot run, ride a bike. If you cannot ride a bike, go for a walk.

And while we are discussing the greater population's general lack of activity, think about pausing the exercise arm that keeps feeding your face, at least from time to time.

For many people …doing arm curls with snacks and beverages represents all the exercise they do!

Work

Work is that thing we do to earn money.

To pay our bills.

To have somewhere comfortable to live, buy food, clothes, and so on.

We are not married to our work, but we work whenever we are awake and there happens to be work that needs to be attended to. For sure, we do not have typical working hours, like 9-5.

It is perfectly fine for average people to be dedicated and committed to the work that they do, and to perform that work to the absolute best of their ability. After all, that is what they are getting paid to do.

But remember this: you cannot sell your job!

If you decide to quit or if you get laid off, you will find yourself simply looking for another job. This is acceptable and describes most people, and we have been conditioned to accept this as the norm.

And to be fair, not every person is meant to be a self-employed entrepreneur, because otherwise there would be no employees!

Most people in developed nations sell their services to employers in exchange for cash.

The people who purchase and pay for human labor, typically create, and own most of the wealth. This is an indisputable fact. The people who create content, products, services, and objects that other people consume are generally the most successful and financially wealthy people on the planet.

If you are a rock star, it is because you make music that people enjoy, and are willing to purchase.

If you created a software program or an app that has been downloaded millions of times, you are probably generating good income today and more potential, future, passive income.

And if your business - regardless of whether founded or acquired by you - serves hundreds or thousands of paying clients, you are probably earning respectable revenue in exchange for the products or services you provide. This probably represents very solid, regular income.

In my examples above, the people who purchase your product (music), use your software, or subscribe to the services you offer, are your paying customers.

To create these products for others to consume, you might have to hire people to help you to make and bring the products to market. Or to service the clients after they had purchased your product.

*****

Most wealthy people have multiple sources of income.

These can be direct earnings - like getting paid for a job - or multiple sources of indirect earnings.

This comment above could be a chapter of this book, or even an entire book on its own.

I referred to passive income above, using an example of someone who had created a software program that people use.

Ideally, software users might pay a relatively small monthly, or annual subscription. Alternatively, the software application could include advertisements, and the owner of the software would earn revenue per click, or commission on any sales executed via the software application. Or a developer could enjoy both, i.e., user fees plus advertising revenue.

This is one type of a passive, secondary income stream.

Similarly, writing a book and selling it, is another example of passive income. Imagine writing one book every two years. This might be a reasonable ask of most people. If you were successful, you might still be earning passive income from your first book, in ten years from today. And by then you would have added four more books to the first one you had authored and published.

This concept can be called an income annuity. That is, income you would start earning once your book starts selling. Income annuity is a fancy term for payment you will receive in perpetuity. It continues for as long as you are alive and even beyond (to your heirs).

The most common example of passive income - for most people - is probably income derived from their investments in stocks or bonds.

A well balanced and diversified equity investment portfolio

serves a twofold purpose for retirees, who are likely to be more risk averse than younger investors: (1) the ever-increasing value of good equity investments - over time - helps to prevent a loss in one's investment portfolio value, and (2) investors receive and rely on regular dividend payouts from the issuer, usually received on a quarterly basis.

An exceptionally good dividend yield might be as high as 10%, annually. These extremely rewarding equity investments are usually Limited Partnerships of some sort.

Master Limited Partnerships in the energy sector frequently pay out high dividends. But one must do research and homework to determine whether such an extraordinary dividend could be considered *safe*, because an issuer can cut, or even cancel a dividend entirely, at any time.

If an investment as described above delivers a 10% annual return, any growth in the share price would be a bonus. Debbie and I own a few of these high-paying dividend stocks.

Some investors prefer fixed income securities.

These securities pay investors fixed interest or dividend payments until it reaches a maturity date. Then, at maturity, the investors are repaid the principal amount they had invested. The most common examples of fixed-income products are government and corporate bonds.

*****

Owning a business is one of the most extraordinary ways to generate passive income, for various reasons.

-     A business can be entirely managed by an absentee owner, or part-time owner. Franchises are great examples of absentee ownership. There are many franchisees who own multiple fast-food restaurants. I have a friend who owns 17 Subway sandwich shops. Obviously, she cannot work at 17 businesses on a regular basis, in person. And if she were to generate only $1,000 per store in passive income, monthly, these restaurants would generate more than $200,000 of passive income earned, per year!

- A business owner enjoys several indirect benefits, as a reward for putting their capital at risk. Many expenses that average, working people pay out of pocket, can be viewed as business expenses for entrepreneurs. As an employee, you might have to pay ongoing expenses in your personal capacity. These expenses might be necessary, like a car (and its related upkeep and maintenance), or a cellphone so that you can be connected to your friends and family on a regular basis. Both examples above are typical, common, business expenses that can be deducted from the business' gross income, for tax purposes, within reason.

Major drawbacks, or negative connotations to business ownership include, to name but a few:

- Endless legislative compliance requirements, at local, state, and federal level.
- Having to put personal capital at risk or borrowing money that must be repaid.
- Managing people, landlords, suppliers, inventory, intangible assets, etc.
- Incurring ongoing predictable costs… in the absence of predictable revenue.
- Competition from similar businesses and new entrants (think taxi ownership vs. Uber).
- Natural disasters like storms, earthquakes, or power outages.
- Man-made threats to the business, including riots, looting and theft.
- Macro-economic risks like a pandemic, changes in taxation

or labor laws (like minimum pay)

Work, for wealthy people, encompasses many aspects of the narratives shared above.

In a previous chapter I mentioned that employees earn a gross salary, taxes are withheld, and the employee gets to keep whatever is left over, after tax.

Entrepreneurs generate gross revenue, pay expenses (including themselves), and pay tax on whatever is left over.

Another critical difference between employees and business owners is how they think. I also described this concept earlier, using the example of a canary yellow Bentley.

In summary, poor people say, "I cannot afford it".

Rich people ask themselves, "How will I afford it?"

These two sentences above illustrate a difference in mindset, when comparing *poor people* to *rich people*, that includes many things that can be taught.

I have personally coached many young children in underprivileged or lower-income areas.

They get it. Perhaps not all of them, but many. And even at an early age, like middle schoolers. They learn, participate, and absorb information that will be useful in the future.

Teaching kids to know how money works offers measurable outcomes, that lead to better futures, often for their families also. I have had countless parents join in on discussions about an introduction to money management, because our education systems have failed them badly.

The rich know how money works, and especially, how to make money work for them.

Even more importantly, wealthy people generally know how

taxes work.

And if you hear complaints about some rich guy who did not pay any taxes, keep in mind that he did not write the tax code. The politician that you had helped to get elected, wrote the tax code that might have benefited the rich guy, and punished you.

In the news, we frequently hear about successful companies - like Amazon - that do not pay any tax. Of course, this is hopelessly untrue, but the media loves to perpetrate myths and fake news.

In 2020, Amazon employed more than 800,000 people.

Of these employees, more than half a million were employed in the United States. I am not certain what the corporation's total payroll costs and taxes were, but the employee portion plus the employer's portion of payroll taxes alone, would be an astronomically huge amount of money.

Even if 500,000 people in the US earned only $20,000 each on an annual basis, that already exceeds $10 billion in payroll expenses, annually. From that total, payroll taxes are withheld, and employer payroll taxes are added.

The understated payroll-related tax expense example above does not yet even scratch the surface of all the other legislatively required business taxes, property taxes, vehicle taxes, business licenses, permits, tariffs and duties payable, *worker's compensation tax* and other employee required insurance-related taxes (e.g., health and safety), the *minimum wage tax* in effect from time to time, financial penalties for legislative infringements, etc.

And you thought CNN was being honest when they reported that Amazon had not paid any tax?

In fact, many employees are not even aware that an employer must pay payroll taxes for the privilege of being able to have that employee work for their business.

A significant failure of our education system is that schools teach success, not failure. The entire system requires memory skills, without critical thinking.

It is almost as if the schools are hellbent on making sure students are uninformed, and able to memorize only what the educators have deemed as necessary information... required for these young adults to become good, reliable, and obedient employees.

*****

EPILOGUE

Not content with an ongoing economic pandemic, that had been replaced by a coronavirus pandemic, which itself had intermittantly been replaced by a racial equity and other pandemics... the *great unwashed* took to the streets from time to time to enjoy some protesting, often accompanied by random acts of rioting, and looting.

Everyone had seemingly, conveniently forgotten about the virus, and *"you are all gonna die."*

In the meanwhile - since hitting a bottom on March 23^{rd,} 2020 - the Dow, and the stock market in general, had been going up and down like a bride's nighty for a few months.

Commentators and pundits on TV argued about different letters of the alphabet, in their attempts to best describe the economic recovery that was meant to follow the recession.

Descriptions like V-, L- or a W-shaped recovery became part of everyday speech for talking heads on financial TV shows.

In an investment environment like this, if you had lost 50% and then regained 50% on an investment, you would still be down 25%. This is quite simple math, rather than talking-head *alphabet soup* or something that requires an abacus to calculate.

Some major banks, like Wells Fargo, had lost half of their market valuations. Many blue-chip stocks had plunged 30-50% from all-time stock price highs achieved, just 4 months prior.

Politicians were proverbially all getting their *knickers in a knot.*

They had no idea how to respond to the pandemic, stock market crashes, ongoing protests, random riots, looting and destruction, and other exciting events.

And today, they still have no idea.

And we, the people, have no idea when this might end.

People in power are saying things like *build back better*, and *you will own nothing, and you will be happy.*

But they did not ask me for my opinion, and I have still not properly learned how to walk on water... excluding in Canada, in winter.

Hopefully, my failings and learnings will be of value to you, as you find your preferred lane... and soar!

If I - as someone with some twenty years of hands-on experience being homeless - can learn financial self-sufficiency and sustainability without receiving a regular paycheck for my daily grind... then so can you!

Onwards and upwards!

*****

PART THREE

TIPS FROM THE INVESTMENT TRENCHES

"Wall Street"

CHAPTER 12

MY OWN LEMONADE STAND

I had started investing in publicly traded equities during my working career, spanning more than two decades. During this time, as a self-directed, retail investor, I made many errors, but I also enjoyed great successes.

Soon, my average monthly, part-time stock market earnings exceeded my earned, monthly salary.

One of the most important philosophies about investing I learned along the way, is that losses are limited to the amount invested. One might lose everything. Therefore, do not invest money that you cannot afford to lose!

However, the flip side of the statement above is that gains are - relatively speaking - limitless or uncapped. In a diversified portfolio, you will always have a few losers. But you only need one 20-bagger, or great performing equity, to right-size a portfolio.

Or just one or two stocks that deliver a 10x or 20x return on the original invested amount will make any investment portfolio look like a winner.

Here is a simple table to illustrate the concepts above:

Equity	Year 1	Year 2	Year 3
A	$10,000	$2,000	$1,000
B	$10,000	$50,000	$75,000
C	$10,000	$10,000	$10,000
Portfolio Value	**$30,000**	**$62,000**	**$86,000**

This table illustrates new, initiated positions in three equities.

- Year 1: My investments were equal $10,000 positions in each stock, respectively.
- Year 2: A had lost nearly all its value | B increased 5x | C was going nowhere
- Year 3: A was close to bankruptcy | B was doing great | C remained flat

Of course, this is an oversimplification of the points I am making, but I am sure you get the picture.

Like many employers, my employers along the way also offered retirement savings plans.

An employer contribution - or match - was a bonus not to be ignored. Effectively, *free money*.

Employer retirement benefit plans are typically institutionally managed. Most, if not all the plan providers, offer employees a listing of mutual funds to select from. Employees typically make ongoing retirement saving contributions via payroll deductions, so it is relatively easy to contribute.

Despite a lack of investment choices (i.e., limited to a list of mutual funds along with their nosebleed fees), investing in an employer-sponsored retirement plan is a good idea.

In addition to free money offered via an employer match, the employees are usually also able to defer taxes to a future date.

The latter allows for more growth, because the actual amount of invested capital would be greater (including the employee's deferred, taxable portion).

Like most employees, I had no idea what the respective mutual funds were investing my money into, because I never bothered to read their respective fund prospectuses.

I would review the list of available mutual funds, and pick one that might have had an important, or serious sounding name, like "Global Equity Growth Fund". I might have looked at the little table that showed the fund's returns over the previous few years... and that was where my savings went.

Hey, it was still better than putting money into a savings account at a bank.!

Human Resource managers are usually unable to offer much assistance and/or financial guidance. This might be a good thing! I am sure they probably followed the same procedure I described above, to pick their funds for personal investment.

Like most people, I had heard success stories about stock market millionaires, and nightmare stories about people who had lost everything they had invested. These were usually about other people's good or bad investment choices, a run of bad luck, or similar.

Sometimes, people would tell stock market horror stories about a guy, who knew a guy, who knew another guy...

But I wanted to learn.

I also wanted to see if it were possible not to lose money... at all.

The Buffet rules: 1. do not lose money and 2. do not forget rule number 1.

It is indeed possible to invest and reduce and/or mitigate the risk of large losses, and I am now going to attempt to share some of my learnings with you.

Some of the chapters that follow were written nearly ten years ago. At the time, I blogged my learning and experiences. I thought that writing things down would prove useful to others. They would be able to avoid my mistakes, copy my successes, or just learn from countless hours that I had spent analyzing, and trying to figure out the gray amorphous mass we refer to as "the market".

I revisited some of my documented experiences and updated the content for this book.

In terms of investing in the stock market, there are a few rules to keep in mind that are as important as the Buffet rules above, and that would be true most of the time:

1. You will not lose money unless you sell the equity you had invested in, for a realized loss. If you purchase company ABC's stock for $10/share and sell it for $5/share, you will have a realized loss of 50%. Conversely, if ABC's stock is trading at $5.00 and you take no action, you will not lose any money unless you sell at that price. In this simple example, if your position were down by 50% you might have to make one of two choices: (a) do nothing, or (b) buy more at the newly discounted price, while the stock is *on sale*.

2. If you had invested $1,000 in ABC, for example, when it was trading at $10/share, your maximum downside risk would be $1,000. You cannot lose more than the entire amount of your investment. Period. In other words, any potential loss is capped at the original amount of your investment. Furthermore, if you cannot afford to invest $1,000 in ABC's stock (or any other), or the $1,000 investment represents money that you might need within the next few months... then you probably should not be investing your money in the stock market.

3. The opposite of number 2. above is true for the upside.

This is entirely uncapped. If the stock of ABC grows to $100/share in the future, then your upside will only be capped if you exit the position (sell the stock) at that point. If you exit at $100/share, you would have generated a 10x return on your investment, before tax. If ABC's stock - in the future - were to trade at $1,000/share... too bad, because you no longer own it! This would be true for people who invested into the startup we know as Amazon at $2/share. At the time of writing (September 2021), Amazon's stock was trading at nearly $3,500/share. To be fair, if you got in at $2/share and exited "too early" at $100/share, you would probably have been incredibly happy anyway, especially on the day you sold your shares for a very handsome profit.

4. The benefit of diversification for an average investor is risk mitigation. Instead of allocating your entire investment to ABC, you buy a mix (or basket/index) of equities. For example, across a few verticals like energy, retail, technology, financial services, etc. It would be less risky to own ABC plus - for example, Exxon, Walmart, Microsoft, and Wells Fargo - than it would be to own stock of company ABC only. The opposite of diversification is a concentrated position. If you have all - or too much - of your portfolio invested in the stock of company ABC, that is a concentrated position, as explained in more detail, in Chapter 12.

In the next few chapters, I will explain some of these concepts in more detail.

If you are already familiar with the topic of one chapter, then just skip to the next.

I am confident that you will derive some benefit, even if reading only one of the chapters that follow becomes viewed as time well spent.

*****

CHAPTER 13

FINANCIAL INSTRUMENTS

Financial instruments are divided into two categories.

The value of cash instruments is determined by the market.

"The market" is governed by supply and demand, as people buy and sell (or trade) various financial instruments.

Cash instruments can further be divided into *securities* and *other securities*, like loans and deposits.

Derivative instruments simply imply that the value of the instrument is derived from something else. Most commonly, the value of the derivative is derived from the value and characteristics of another entity, like an asset, interest rate or index. Derivatives can further be divided into *exchange-traded derivatives* and *over the counter* (OTC) derivatives, describing how they are traded.

The descriptions above may sound overly complicated but are not really that complex. However, trading in many of these different instruments are often overly complex, especially for a novice investor.

Here are a few simple and relatively common examples of the 4 financial instruments described above:

1. Securities include bonds, stocks, and T-Bills (or Treasury Bills). Securities can also include commercial paper, also called promissory notes. Bonds, much like T-Bills and commercial paper, are instruments of indebtedness by the bond issuer to the bond holders. These are therefore called *debt* securities. Stock in an incorporated business, on the other hand, constitutes *equity*.

2. Other securities are generally limited to loans, deposits, certificates of deposit, and FX-spot (foreign exchange) rates. Although the latter may be a term people are least familiar with, the average daily turnover of global FX spot transactions exceeds US$2 trillion.

3. Exchange-traded securities include bonds, stock, equity, and currency *futures*. Futures simply imply that parties agree to buy or sell a specified asset for a price agreed upon today (the strike price) with delivery & payment occurring at a future date (the delivery date).

4. OTC derivatives are like exchange-traded securities, but also include interest rate and currency swaps, caps & floors, and options.

You may have heard of calls and puts: These are short names for call options and put options.

Your options contracts give you the right to buy or sell an underlying instrument. You buy the underlying at a certain price, called a strike price, and you pay a premium to buy it.

Some other derivatives - like stock options and restricted stock awards - are generally most used as an integral part of executive compensation plans.

As a rule, stock award plans serve a dual purpose: (1) they encourage employees to think and behave like owners, because that is what they are - or become - by owning shares of the company they work for; and (2) it helps the company to attract, and retain, talented employees.

*****

CHAPTER 14

A CONCENTRATED POSITION

A concentrated position occurs when an investor owns shares of a stock (or other security type) that represents a large percentage of his or her overall portfolio. The investor's wealth therefore becomes concentrated in a single position.

According to R.W. Baird (a wealth management company), depending on the volatility of the stock, and the size of the client's portfolio, a position is often considered to be concentrated when it represents 10% or more of one's entire investment portfolio.

We probably all have family, friends or colleagues who have an investment portfolio heavily concentrated in one particular asset class. They may hold a concentrated equity position in their employer's stock for several reasons, for example:

-    A lack of knowledge and/or experience in asset diversification

-    A lack of knowledge regarding general investment risk management

-    Lack of liquidity to acquire other assets, i.e., buying company stock in small quantities that add up over time, e.g., via a share purchase program offered by their employer

-    A feeling that they know their employer's business better than any other business, and that owning the employer's stock is therefore less risky than investments in other equities

- Personal emotion related to control and/or a sense of belonging: for example, the more of my company's stock I own, the more obvious my commitment to the business, the lesser my risk of termination, better my chances of promotion, etc.

Family wealth created by holding a single stock that appreciates substantially in value over time is common.

For example, senior company executives may receive stock or stock options as part of their compensation, investors benefit from superior appreciation of one stock relative to the rest of their portfolio, or family members inherit a large position in a single stock.

Regardless of how the concentrated position is acquired, it results in a disproportionate allocation of wealth, which exposes the family to undue risk that should be understood and managed.

Whether investors understand the risks of holding a concentrated position or not, there is a tendency to hold onto these positions.

Corporate executives may also face insider selling constraints or concerns about how a sale would affect the market price of their company's stock.

In the marketplace, senior managers, and executives (especially insiders) who buy their employer's stock are viewed positively, while insider selling causes people to be concerned.

Simply put:

- Insider buying shows confidence in the company's future performance, expected financial results, etc. or maybe some knowledge of a potential big, positive news release that prompted the purchase; but

- Insider selling, on the other hand, makes investors feel uncomfortable. If the CEO is selling, why would I want to maintain my position? In this latter example, we may be ignoring the fact that the CEO has a concentrated investment position in the company's equity - built up over many years - and that he or she might be wishing to diversify or rebalance their investment portfolio a little.

Quite often, investors simply have an emotional attachment to an equity. For example, people might acquire more and more stock of Tesla, because they really like battery-powered cars. Or they might believe that by driving a Tesla instead of a fossil fuel-powered, combustion engine car, they are saving the planet, or the environment.

Investors are often concerned about the tax implications of selling because a realized gain triggers a tax event. A future tax liability should not be a criterion for not liquidating some of one's equity, if the timing and motivation to do so, fits the investor's financial objectives and requirements.

For example, if an investor were to achieve a 100% gain on a position, the investor might decide to sell half of the position and retain the other half.

The remaining 50% - half of the position that was not sold - would then represent *free money*. The entire position that remains invested, represents *playing with the house's money*.

Of course, the realized gain from the sale of 50% of the original position would trigger a tax event - a tax liability based on the gross value of the gain would become due to the collection agency, and the investor will retain whatever remains after taxes have been deducted.

There might be a critical inflection point for an investor or family office, where the desire for wealth, income and lifestyle preservation outweighs the need for further wealth creation. Very often, wealthy investors and family offices will shift their focus to concessionary social investments - conceding future financial return on investment - or philanthropy, in some form or another.

Today, many philanthropists focus on making social impact investments that may generate a financial return on investment, or not, subject to their individual purpose, objectives, values and/or mission.

If you have a concentrated position in your personal investment portfolio, you might want to speak to an investment advisor. It would be good to explore a risk mitigation plan, and some investment diversification that will be better suited to your beneficiaries in the medium- to longer term.

There are several advisors who specialize in helping investors to exit concentrated positions. Find one best suited and address this common investment challenge while you can do so.

"The chance of gain is by every man more
or less overvalued, and the chance of loss
is by most men undervalued"

- Adam Smith, Wealth of Nations

*****

CHAPTER 15

THE RELATIVITY OF FINANCIAL RISK

Too much gold… too much cash… too great a holding in your employer's stock…

Diversification is as old as investing itself. At its most basic definition, diversification simply means that you should diversify your investments over a few different asset classes, rather than just one, or a few.

Many US homeowners lost all their equity (assuming they had any to begin with) during the housing market collapse of 2008/9. The simple math behind this investment dilemma is that homeowners *bought more house* than they needed, and for more money than what they were able to afford… with the bank's money.

Buyers were making stupid decisions, supported by greedy realtors and bankers!

How could you lose "all your equity" on a residential home, you may ask? Well, you may have been able to purchase a house with a 3% down payment. Or, you might have put down a deposit of 30% of your hard earned, saved cash.

Either way, you did not buy the home - the party that contributed the balance of the purchase price that you did not have, bought the house, and you rented it from that financier (the mortgage company, or bank).

Anytime a 3rd party has the legal right to repossess *your property* - for example, due to non-payment of debt - you did not own that property to begin with.

Also, you might have bought a house and you were required to pay $x monthly for the mortgage, $y for annual property tax, and $z for upkeep and maintenance. If this were true, you did not own an asset... but a recurring, ongoing, monthly liability!

This is a critical point. Despite what we learn in accounting class, it is better to think of assets as things that make you money, and liabilities as things that cost you money.

Someone might say, "My house is my greatest asset". You might respond with a question, or at least quietly think to yourself, "How much money do you make on your house, every month?"

If you own a rental home and a tenant who occupies it pays you $1,000 in rent, per month, your house might be an asset. I say might because I am assuming that the property taxes and any costs paid by the owner, is less than the rent. Otherwise, that rental home is also a liability.

In Accounting verbiage, buildings, machinery, cars, etc. are all viewed as assets. In life, these physical property items are only assets if they are making you money.

As I write this, my family owns an office condo that we use for our business purposes, for ourselves. We own the property free and clear - in other words, there is no mortgage or other liability attached to our ownership of this physical asset, in accounting terms.

We pay condo dues, property taxes, utilities, etc. If you were to ask me what this asset is worth, I would explain that it is a liability, because it is costing our family $x per month. It might become an asset if we sold it for cash, for example, but until that date, the office condo is a liability.

Of course, on my balance sheet, the office condo is listed as an asset.

The comparison above illustrates the difference between understanding *bookkeeping for tax purposes* vs. a personal *understanding of assets and liabilities*.

These two words - assets and liabilities - are two of the most misunderstood words in financial literacy, mainly due to commonly accepted Accounting-language verbiage.

Another two words that - along with an understanding of assets and liabilities - create a foundation for financial literacy, are cash flow.

If you can absolutely understand *assets, liabilities, and cash flow*, you are on a path to financial success, and independence:

- Assets are things that make you money (e.g., your car, if you drive for Uber)

- Liabilities are things that cost you money (e.g., your car, while parked in the garage)

- Incoming cash flows should exceed outgoing cash flows, measured over a realistic, logical period.

*****

The stock market has been up and down, frequently by >1% in one day. 'High yielding' bonds have been delivering low yields. Employees lose their jobs and are then unable to find replacement jobs, let alone similar-paying jobs. There is a general lack of political will and direction from elected *leaders*.

People *overinvest* in one investment vehicle, activity, category, or sector. For example, their job!

Add all the above together... and you end up with a recipe for an awful minestrone of volatility and fear!

Employees of publicly traded companies often benefit from buying their employers' stock at a discount or may even be given stock in lieu of cash. This is generally a great deal!

These stock awards and savings plans range from large, publicly traded companies that offer their employees discounts - e.g., 15% off the market value of the company's stock - to startups that have no money and end up offering their employees company stock in lieu of cash compensation.

The concepts immediately above are attractive to most employees. Unfortunately, many average members of the so-called middle class then end up owning too much of their employer's stock AND living in a house - for which they overpaid - that is really owned by the bank.

Together, these two investment vehicles above may represent a somewhat diversified investment strategy: equity + property.

But the employee may inadvertently have ended up in a concentrated position: a concentrated position in the equity of his or her employer *plus* an ongoing liability of a large portion of monthly income used for paying *rent* to the mortgage lender of the house they live in.

How to diversify then?

Firstly, debt is the classic middle-class trap - student loans, home loans, credit card debt, car loans, etc. Get rid of it. Especially the high interest debt first, like credit card debt.

Secondly, you can manage yourself out of concentrated positions.

If you own too much of your employer's stock, sell some and move that cash elsewhere, e.g., into other stocks. If you live in a mortgaged house and you are servicing debt that costs e.g., more than 30% of your after-tax income, get out of that concentrated liability by downsizing, renting out a basement room, refinancing, etc.

If you are living beyond your ongoing positive cash flow or financial means, just stop! If you do not know how to stop, or need assistance, then find someone to help you get out of your negative cash flow spiral.

This is the greatest financial risk; causing one to run the risk of not being able to service debt, should circumstances change unexpectedly!

There is no singular safe investment. Cash declines daily, even if only due to inflation.

Gold - *with fundamentals based almost entirely on shiny* - is only a haven until the next gold price crash. Equities are volatile, constantly going up and down. *Safe paper investments* (treasuries, municipal bonds, etc.) offer returns commensurate with bank savings accounts, i.e., almost nothing.

Work to create a truly diversified investment position, mixing some property with equities, cash, and other investments (anything of appreciating value). Maybe allocate 5-10% of your portfolio to a gold ETF? Perhaps consider reducing the cash position of your asset portfolio to 10-15% of total value?

By now, many people have figured out that the *American Dream*, with its foundation built on homeownership, is a myth. The reason for this is not the home, but the mortgage required by most people to purchase that home.

A mortgage is a product that was invented by banks, to sell loans to consumers. Banks would go out of business if they only accepted deposits.

Over time, politicians and other community leaders bought into the concept of the American Dream and started co-promoting the bankers' mortgage products.

Having a mortgage locks most lenders into a debt spiral for most of their working lives. It eliminates - or at least negatively impacts - their mobility to explore opportunities elsewhere. Not only in other cities, but also in other countries.

The worst feature of a debt trap is that mortgages - the way the system is setup – are designed to encourage consumers to purchase housing they cannot afford, to impress people they do not know.

If you are reading this book in the living room of the house you live in, that you purchased with a down payment of 20-30%, you must realize that the bank owns more of the *asset* than you. Which means, in real terms, that you are living in their house, and paying a high rental for the use of their 70-80% ownership of your property you maintain, pay taxes on, repair, beautify, etc.

There is always only one winner.

The mortgagor or mortgagee.

Not both.

*****

CHAPTER 16

TRAILING STOPS

Earlier on, I mentioned that I wanted to learn if, or how, it would be near impossible to lose money on the stock market. Using trailing stops to protect gains and mitigate against stock market losses, is a methodology that I have used consistently for more than a decade.

A trailing stop is an order entered with a stop parameter that creates a trailing or moving activation price.

What does that mean?

Example # 1: You bought a company's stock for $10. That stock is currently trading at $15/share. You enter a 3% *trailing stop sell order*. If the stock were to fall by 3% from the current $15/share price (i.e., it goes down by about $0.50), the trailing stop order will execute a sell order for $14.50, locking in your $4.50/share profit.

✓ In a bull market, when stocks are going up... you effectively will not lose money using this methodology, although it is possible that you may have been able to achieve a greater gain without the trailing stop order executing (commonly aka greed)!

✓ When the bears pounce and stocks decline in value... you

will limit your losses - if any - within a set percentage or dollar range that you have pre-determined and are comfortable with!

Example # 2: As the price for the stock moves up, the activation price (for the sell order) will **trail** the new, higher value. Using my same "$10 buy / $15 current" example above, if the stock were to move from $15/share to $18/share over a period, the trailing stop order will trail the increased price over that same period, e.g., becoming 3% of $18 (= $0.60/share). This means that if the $18/share stock were to lose about $0.60/share in value - having fallen from its bid price of $18/share, the trailing stop order will be activated, becoming a market order at a sale price of $17.40/share. Your gain will be $7.40/share, on your original $10/share purchase price.

Example # 3: Stocks also go down in value. So, conversely, if you had bought the stock at $10/share and this stock is currently trading at $8/share, you could enter e.g., the same 3% trailing stop sell order to mitigate your risk of losing more of your investment. If the price for the $8/share stock declined by about $0.25, it would trigger the sell and your position will be closed at around $7.75/share, limiting potential further financial loss.

*****

Why should we use a trailing stop sell order?

Firstly, to help manage and control your investor emotion! Secondly, for long positions (where you intend to own the shares for a while), this technology - provided by your online broker - will help maximize and protect your profit in rising markets, and limit your losses in falling markets... and everyone would like to achieve that, right?

An illustration, courtesy TD Ameritrade:

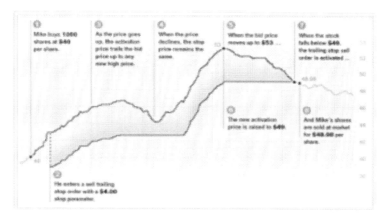

Be sure to explore and become familiar with these (and other) technology tools that are often available at no cost to investors... tools that will assist you in managing your investor emotion and help you in your quest to achieve a maximum return on your investments!

*****

CHAPTER 17

A TRAILING STOP CASE STUDY - BOEING, BOEING, GONE

You do NOT absolutely want to be in a position where you rely entirely on someone else to manage your hard-earned money! Basic investment knowledge is a must have!

In fact, passing e.g., a Series 7 (U.S. Certification) test to become a licensed Financial Advisor is no different to passing e.g., a realtor certification test, thereby becoming a licensed realtor. This is not a disparaging comment, but simply a statement of fact. A license from some formal authority does not qualify a person as an expert, or as someone who cares about your financial well-being, or even proves subject matter expertise and/or knowledge... beyond that which was required for passing the test.

You must be able to manage and/or understand your investments... otherwise, you will be more likely to lose money somewhere along the line... regardless of whom you may reward with your trust (not to mention, your cash!).

On July 12, 2013, Boeing shares had opened for trading at $106.86/share. I know this for two reasons: (1) I looked it up and (2) I was long $BA (meaning I owned Boeing shares) that were sold that day.

I had not planned to close my position (sell my shares). In fact, my $BA shares were showing a gain of around 40% YTD... so I just loved my Boeing stock!

When I had an opportunity to visit Seattle for business, I even visited both Boeing museums, talked to retired Boeing engineers at the exhibits to learn more about the company, marveled and played with the technology on display, and more.

I know, right... what a geek!

I had opened the position above on January 30, 2013, at $74.54/share.

It closed - note: I did not say *"I closed the position, but rather that "it closed"* automatically - via 3% automated Trailing Stop, at a sell price of $104.81/share.

Why?

Boeing stock was cruising along quite nicely at a respectable altitude until around noon on July 12, 2013.

News broke about a cockpit fire on a new Ethiopian Boeing 787 Dreamliner, that caused the shares to suddenly plummet.

By 12:30 pm, $BA was trading at $99.40/share. From this new low for the day the price could have gone down further. It did not, and even recovered a little, to close at around $102.

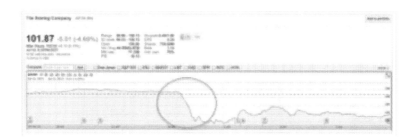

What could possibly be wrong, booking a 40% gain on an investment in just over 5 months? You might offer that I now had a tax liability that would cut my realized gain considerably.

And I may counter with "so what"?

With the portion of the realized gain that I get to keep - after taxes - I could reinvest in $BA, or any other equity that will deliver a return on investment commensurate with my investment objectives, expectations, and financial plan.

Because I sold the shares for a profit, I can also buy back into $BA right away. If I had sold my investment at a loss and reopened a position immediately, it would be a wash sale. I would not have been able to book the loss as a reduction of personal income for tax purposes in this scenario.

Boeing is a great company to invest in. The corporation will probably continue to offer stellar returns in the future, especially once the 787 Dreamliner bugs have been addressed and eliminated, and as airline companies all over the world start and/or continue to replace their aging fleets.

For now, I am out of my $BA position, and I did not even have to think about it. As soon as the stock had declined 3% off its intraday high of $108.13, my 3% Trailing Stop automatically became an executable market order, closing in real time at $104.81... and booking my 40%+ gain as a reward for 5 months of investment risk in a blue-chip Dow stock.

No fancy stuff... no puts, covered call options, timing the market, etc. Just a simple, easy-to-use technology tool that automatically executed a sale... while I was out hitting some golf balls at an indoor practice driving range during my lunch hour!

*****

April 2020 update: As I was writing this, $BA stock was trading at around $150.00/share. In March 2019 - a year prior - $BA stock traded at around $440.00/share.

This highlights a few market-related observations:

- Even large, blue-chip stocks like Boeing are subject to massive price fluctuations.

- If I had held my long position in Boeing shares - opened at $75/share in 2013 - when it hit a high of $440/share in 2019, I would have had an unrealized gain (on paper) of nearly 6x my original investment.

- Without a trailing stop, with a "buy-and-hold" investment strategy, my unrealized gain would have been 2x the original invested amount in 2020, compared with a 6x multiple, just one year prior.

- If I had plugged in a 5% trailing stop as the price was going up (to $440/share), my position would have sold out, or closed, at around $420/share for a 560% taxable gain, realized over about 6 years (2013-2019) *

* In real terms, I use trailing stops on a regular basis to protect my gains. In the Boeing examples shared above, I would have been more likely to have opened and closed positions in Boeing stock several times during the 6-year period illustrated above.

Typically, as soon as I have a position with a 25-30% unrealized gain, I plug in a 3-5% trailing stop. Generally, when my trailing stops execute to become sell orders, I first keep the realized cash for some time, before buying back into the same, or any other equities. This strategy also helps me to avoid catching the proverbial falling knife, because one cannot predict, guess, or assume the bottom of an equity's sudden decline in value.

*****

CHAPTER 18

WHAT IS AN ETF?

People invest in many different types of vehicles, or investment instruments. In this chapter we will briefly explore an ETF and compare it to an alternative investment choice.

ETF = **E**xchange **T**raded **F**und

ETFs are equity investments that are traded just like other company equity on a stock exchange, e.g. the NYSE.

The key elements included in this short description are that an ETF can be traded like stock (i.e. via an online brokerage account), and - perhaps more importantly - that an ETF is a fund... not dissimilar to a mutual fund or any other 'basket' of investments, grouped together for investment purposes.

An ETF therefore holds a variety of assets like stocks, commodities, or bonds.

These funds then typically track or mimic another, or broader market index, such as the Dow Jones Industrial Index (commonly called the Dow).

The Dow is widely recognized as a primary benchmark of the day's stock market activity. All over the world people would often use the terms *the market* and *the Dow* synonymously, when describing a day's activity on the stock market.

Even in other countries - I have lived and worked in a few different countries - people refer to the Dow as an economic indicator when they talk about the market moving higher, or lower.

Unlike owning stocks - for which the only, one-time fee might be brokerage commission paid at the time of purchase - ETF investments are typically subject to annual management and other fees.

However, ETF fees are generally lower than comparative fund investment instruments, like mutual funds.

Investors who trade ETFs are trading their shares on a secondary market, as opposed to owning the issuer's equity directly.

ETFs have been available in the US for about 20 years.

In 1998, State Street Global Advisors issued an ETF for investment, called SPDR Dow Jones Industrial Average, traded under the ticker symbol "DIA". I picked this one as an example, because it will allow me to compare DIA to the Dow, which itself is a basket and index of 30 U.S. whales.

One can view the Dow issuers via a Google search of "Dow 30 stocks", or similar. The 30 issuers that make up the Dow index changes from time to time.

The basket of stocks included in DIA is described in the fund's prospectus, which you can retrieve and download from the issuer's website. Their top fund holdings include these Dow heavyweights:

In April 2020, the DIA ETF held these top 10 equity positions and weightings:

UnitedHealth Group Incorporated, 8.70%

Apple Inc., 8.35%

Home Depot Inc., 5.82%
McDonald's Corporation, 5.23%
Goldman Sachs Group Inc., 5.16%
Microsoft Corporation, 5.16%
Visa Inc. Class A, 4.73%
Johnson & Johnson, 4.36%
3M Company, 4.22%
Boeing Company, 3.91%

Any investors could mimic DIA (in other words you could buy the same stocks as the super smart fund managers at State Street), without having to pay any fees (other than one-time brokerage commission when you buy the stock).

The fund holdings listed above gross up to around 55% of the DIA fund's total investments (we did not investigate the other 45%).

Remember that State Street has skilled traders who can open and close positions (buy and sell stocks) quickly and expertly, and who are using smarter trading tools than amateur investors have, etc. \

One could therefore argue that paying a low annual fee may be worthwhile for the expertise State Street Advisors offer in managing your investment (according to the Morningstar Investor Research website, State Street's fees for DIA is inexpensive at <0.5% annually).

So, let us assume you have $10,000 available for investment. You could buy about 40 shares of DIA (current price ~$240), or you could buy, for example, $1,000 worth of shares in each of the fund's top ten holdings above (respectively) and end up more or less in the same place.

The difference on an ongoing basis would be nominal but may become significant over the longer term.

There are pros and cons on both sides of the equation: If you buy

DIA, you only make one purchase, but you incur a nominal on-going 'fund management' fee.

If you were to buy the 10 different stocks directly you would own them outright after paying brokerage commissions (no future fees). But... you would then be required to manage your investments and pay attention to your investments to mitigate financial loss in the longer term.

Many people would prefer to have a professional fund manager doing this on their behalf, especially at minimal ongoing cost. However, even a minimal fee compounded, e.g. over 20 years, adds up to an amount of lost savings that could be considered material to your investment portfolio value in the future.

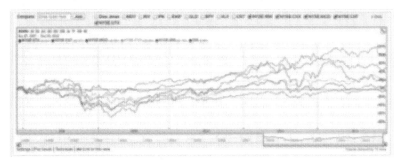

On the graph above I compared the performance of DIA vs. 5 Dow stocks for the previous 5 years. The DIA performance is reflected by the line at the bottom. The 5 Dow stocks were selected because of recent mixed performance. What is observationally interesting is that all the stocks, along with DIA, follow the same pattern in the graph.

What is more important is that the 30 stocks that make up the Dow have collectively, consistently delivered about 6-7% year over year, for a lot longer than 100 years. This average includes major events that had impacted the stock market, e.g., pre-war recession, 9/11 events, the 2008/09 financial market meltdown, the 2020 coronavirus depression, etc.

So, instead of having cash safely tucked away under your mattress or in a bank savings account, you should know that you could have a consistent return of around 7% by simply investing in a basket of Dow stocks, longer term.

I am confident that this beats the return paid by your bank on savings accounts!

However, three further points of clarification are required:

- find a great company to invest in and buy it - i.e., do not trade these stocks regularly, because if you do, you will likely lose money.

- reinvest all dividends while you are earning an income - i.e., do not withdraw any gains unless you absolutely need the cash; and

- buy when it is red and sell when it is green - i.e., when blue chip stocks go down e.g., because of quarterly results, that is usually a signal to buy; and if the stock you already own is in the red, don't sell unless there's a compelling reason to do so!

The objective is simply never to take a loss, because over the longer term, you never really need to, if you invest in a basket of Dow stocks.

*****

CHAPTER 19

HOW MUCH MONEY DO I NEED TO RETIRE?

So... you are thinking about retirement?

At the risk of getting overly philosophical, maybe we should first explore what retirement means.

Sometimes people say they just want to relax, and I respond by asking "how long will it be before you get bored?" At other times people say they would like to travel, and I respond by asking "and what will you do when you get back?"

But let us assume we are all saving for retirement – which is unconditionally a good idea – and the question is "how much do I need to save in order to retire?"

I am going to start by assuming that the Social Security net is broken, the system is bankrupt, and you must be able to take care of yourself.

By way of an example, I am going to assume net (after tax) household income of $40,000 and monthly expenses of $3,000. Out of the gate, applying simple math, we can deduce that spending $3,000 a month equals $36,000 which, in turn, leaves you able to save $4,000 (or 10% of net income) for discretionary expenses.

Note two important points, in case you missed Chapter 13:

- you must spend less than what you earn; and

- you must save at least 10% of your net income while you are gainfully employed.

All good so far?

Now, the second critical step is to ensure that you have enough cash (or cash equivalents) on hand to be able to cover 12 months of living expenses in the event of a job loss, illness, or other unexpected reason.

This implies that you already have $36,000 - in liquid assets - saved and available... just in case.

Still good?

If not, and you are still reading this... we are already making progress!

Many smart financial advisors - people far smarter than me - suggest that your investment portfolio should include about 10-15% cash (or assets that can quickly be turned into cash, like stocks). This could represent the $36,000 in liquid cash, mentioned above.

If $36,000 equals 10%, then 100% would be $360,000. That is probably a good minimum savings target. Minimum, because - when it comes to money - more is usually better!

But, $360,000 returning approximately 7% will only generate a return of about $25,000 annually.

This means that if you are currently spending $3,000 a month (as per my example above), you will have to cut your expenses by $1,000 a month.

This might be easy, because if you are not working, you will not need to shop for new clothes as often, pay for transport, buy lunch, etc. Or this may be difficult because you are already living a simple life (not shopping much, walking to work, making lunch at home, etc.).

The greatest ongoing cost for most people is rent or a mortgage, and you need a place to live. Can you downsize your living arrangements?

Perhaps the availability of some Social Security benefits (in the future) will add to your monthly income? Could you relocate to a less expensive town/city/country? Could you work part-time in retirement and call yourself semi-retired instead?

Back to the example above: To deliver about $36,000 an investor would need about $500,000 invested, assuming a pre-tax return of 7%. If you can generate a higher return, you can get away with less savings. If you are going to invest in 'safe' securities, like bonds, you will need more savings.

Either way, it is never too late to start saving!

Typical middle-class, salaried employees should NOT contemplate retirement with debt, or having to rely on government support.

If you are currently spending $3,000/month and you are in reach of that initial goal of $360,000 demonstrated above, you are well on your way to self-sufficiency in retirement.

Do not rush to stop working and earning a living and keep saving. When you are ready to relax and enjoy the fruits of your labor... happy retirement!

*****

CHAPTER 20

WHAT ABOUT A VARIABLE ANNUITY?

An important question to ask about annuities, is "How much does a Variable Annuity cost?

You will pay several charges when you invest in a Variable Annuity ("VA").

Often, they will include the following:

- Surrender charges – If you withdraw money from a VA within a certain period after a purchase payment (typically within six to eight years, but sometimes as long as ten years), the insurance company will usually assess a surrender charge, which is a type of "sales charge". This charge is used to pay your financial professional a commission for selling the VA to you. Generally, the surrender charge is a percentage of the amount withdrawn, and declines gradually over a period of several years, known as the "surrender period." For example, a 7% charge might apply in the first year after a purchase payment, 6% in the second year, 5% in the third year, and so on until the eighth year, when the surrender charge no longer applies. Often, contracts will allow you to withdraw part of your account value each year – 10% or 15% of your account value, for example – without paying a surrender charge.

For example: You purchase a VA contract with a $10,000 purchase payment. The contract has a schedule of surrender charges, beginning with a 7% charge in the first year, and declining by 1% each year. In addition, you can withdraw 10% of your contract value each year free of surrender charges. In the first year, you decide to withdraw $5,000, or one-half of your contract value of $10,000 (if your contract value has not increased or decreased because of investment performance). In this case, you could withdraw $1,000 (10% of contract value) free of surrender charges, but you would pay a surrender charge of 7%, or $280, on the other $4,000 withdrawn.

- Mortality and expense risk charge – This charge is equal to a certain percentage of your account value, typically in the range of 1.25% per year. This charge compensates the insurance company for insurance risks it assumes under the annuity contract. Profit from the mortality and expense risk charge is sometimes used to pay the insurer's costs of selling the VA, such as a commission paid to your financial professional for selling the VA to you.

For example: Your VA has a mortality and expense risk charge at an annual rate of 1.25% of account value. Your average account value during the year is $20,000, so you will pay $250 in mortality and expense risk charges that year.

- Administrative fees – The insurer may deduct charges to cover record-keeping and other administrative expenses. This may be charged as a flat account maintenance fee (perhaps $25 or $30 per year) or as a percentage of your account value (typically in the range of 0.15% per year).

For example: Your VA charges administrative fees at an annual rate of 0.15% of account value. Your average account value during the year is $50,000. You will pay $75 in administrative fees.

- Underlying Fund Expenses – You will also indirectly pay the fees and expenses imposed by the mutual funds that are the underlying investment options for your VA.

-    Fees and Charges for Other Features – Special features offered by some variable annuities, such as a stepped-up death benefit, a guaranteed minimum income benefit, or long-term care insurance, often carry additional fees and charges.

Other charges, such as initial sales loads, or fees for transferring part of your account from one investment option to another, may also apply. You should ask your financial professional to explain to you all charges that may apply. You can also find a description of the charges in the prospectus for any VA that you are considering.

Be sure you understand all the charges before you invest. These charges will reduce the value of your account and the return on your investment.

*****

CHAPTER 21

SHOULD YOUR KID GO TO COLLEGE?

Part one: No

Here is my take on a typical U.S. (*insert your country here*) college education:

1. Colleges feature resort-style facilities at prices like luxury beach resorts – send your kid to a beach resort in Dominican Republic; it will cost the same, but she will have more fun, and it will be more educational.

2. The college experience is mostly 'party-time' for young kids, depriving them of quality learning, independent thinking, and general life experience.

3. The lost 'opportunity cost' of attending college can be measured in more than just money (see # 2 above, and # 4 below)

4. The product does not match either the aspirational value, usefulness, or cost of the goods sold, especially when measured in $ return on investment, or ROI.

5. In the past, students were at least taught a sense of entitlement based on learning, future earnings, etc. Today, that value proposition is also gone.

6. Colleges stifle creativity (at a peak during early years). Innovation and new ideas – during a time of abundant availability – are sacrificed, focusing instead on 'book knowledge' about historical events, thoughts, and philosophies.

7. Colleges support the teaching of risk avoidance and mitigation ("you need to graduate to get a good job"). Young people have greater risk tolerance. The older we get, the more risk averse we become.

Let us revisit point # 4 above:

Q: What can one buy for $150,000 (i.e., the average cost of a 4-year degree in the US)?

How about a year spent teaching English to kids in Japan, a turnkey retail business (e.g., the entry cost of a Subway franchise is about $100,000), and about $40,000 in cash 'left over' to fund the first few months of business expenses, if required.

The difference in ROI is not only significant, but also material in terms of breaking the mold young people are coerced into.

The mantra: "get an education, in order to get a job, in order to qualify for a lifetime of middle-class debt" vs. self-employment and – more importantly – sustainable, debt-free, self-sufficiency!

As a small business owner, you will generate an income for yourself and other people. You will employ people who graduated with student debt, like an accountant.

You will have equity and you will start creating wealth on day one – creating assets with value. These assets can be sold, allowing you to buy another business; or leveraged, allowing you to expand your existing business, open a second store, etc.

Some of your kid's high school friends, who went to college, will likely ask your self-employed child for work. She will be unlikely to hire these graduates because they are unlikely to offer any value to the business commensurate with their sense of entitlement, drilled into them at home, and at school!

*****

Part Two: Yes

But only when your child reaches a certain level of maturity and when tertiary education can be funded WITHOUT ANY DEBT. Maturity will obviously differ from child to child, in terms of age, life experience, etc. Very few seventeen-year-olds can think and plan for the rest of their lives. Heck, some adults are still deciding!

A professional degree, e.g., law, medicine, accounting, etc., requires a formal college education, as one should expect. Almost any other degree offers little or no value beyond the personal and life experiences derived, and perhaps especially later in one's career.

Refer to part 1. The answer was no. It assumed to be addressing typical parents of high school children, from typical middle-class families. In other words, people who would typically require debt financing to pay for college. The answer is absolutely "no"!

The opening paragraph above is not a contradiction to the previous no. Debbie and I have two sons, neither of them schooled in the traditions of middle-class America (or Canada, where they were raised).

Our older son finished high school in Canada and left promptly thereafter to teach English in Muikamachi, Japan for a year. The cost of this life education was minimal, at only a few thousand dollars in travel costs and pocket money. To qualify for his teaching post at a kindergarten school, he had completed a TEFL certificate on weekends during his senior year at high school.

When he returned from Japan to Toronto, he enrolled for a general business diploma, part-time at a local college, and worked regular, low-paying retail jobs (just like other students) to help fund his tuition. Occasionally we helped him with some of the tuition and general cost of living expenses. With the $150,000 we saved on full time college tuition, we bought an apartment, which he lived in, that we later sold.

We reinvested some of the proceeds into our family's real estate portfolio, which he co-owns.

Today, he has a professional day job, a wife, and three children. His adventure in Japan probably long forgotten, at least somewhat.

When our younger son was 19, he enrolled at Brighton College (UK), studying online, part-time.

He also worked 5-6 days a week as a driver for a car dealership. It happened to be a Mercedes Benz dealership, which meant that he was also able to enjoy driving some of the finest cars on the planet.

This implies that he might have liked his part-time, low-paying job. He did not, for the most part, but continued working at that dealership while completing, and paying for, his academic studies.

He paid his own tuition, and we helped with some of the cost-of-living expenses.

He still lives in Florida, in a property owned free and clear.

Total student debt = $0.

His current personal investment portfolio has a healthy balance. His investments include blue-chip and other equities, cash, and a couple of ETFs.

Total tuition costs referenced above = less than $10,000 with $0 student debt, as mentioned above.

Sound doable?

I am guessing the answer might be "yes".

*****

CHAPTER 22

DOWNSIZING FOR RETIREMENT

There comes a time in life when it may make sense to downsize!

Children might have grown up, and left home. A spouse may regrettably die. Perhaps an ever-increasing cost of living demands changes to accommodate a lower budgeted income due to retirement, loss of a job, etc.

Of course, there may be more and/or other reasons to consider downsizing. Regardless of the reason, it takes time to plan and manage such a complex process.

If you are retiring and planning to live on income earned from investments, then – more than ever – taking time to calculate and record ongoing expenses to arrive at a monthly budget becomes critical. Remember to also include planning for any unexpected expenses in a monthly budget, like illness, car or home repairs, etc.

If your home has no mortgage owing against it (at retirement age you ideally should not have a mortgage), and you wish to remain in your current home… then you should calculate whether living on your investment income would cover all your living expenses.

Calculate your living expenses by creating a simple spreadsheet. There are many sample budgets available on the Internet, for free.

Make sure to include the cost of food, property tax, assumed maintenance costs, and utilities based on historical costs and expected increases. If your cost of living is higher than your income, it is time to take the next step to downsize so that you can live according to your income.

Ask yourself some tough questions!

Do you really need to live and maintain a huge property? Does the idea of a smaller apartment or condo offer you a chance to downsize your total living expenses? Finding a smaller condo that is e.g., within walking distance to shops can be a huge benefit. Shopping locally may reduce or eliminate the ongoing cost and maintenance required for a car.

An opportunity to save on transportation costs would be complemented by walking as part of a daily routine, offering a good chance at regular, light exercise. Or perhaps you could consider a condo near the beach, offering an opportunity to walk outdoors, and to enjoy the seashore experience!

Selling your existing home and purchasing a smaller home could free up additional funds for investment. Moreover, a smaller property may also offer savings on ongoing utility costs, property taxes and maintenance costs.

Savings AND extra money to invest!

If you decide to keep your property, calculate whether you could offer it for rent to a tenant, with that rent covering the total cost of ownership. Can renting your existing home also cover the cost of a smaller home/apartment for you to live in?

Life is full of choices and retirement planning is all part of the adventure. Whatever you do, do not panic!

Take time and make choices that match your desired lifestyle. Downsizing may also mean more time to do more, with your available time. This may include time to perhaps engage in some part-time work for extra cash, volunteer your services for the benefit of your favorite non-profit and their charitable mission... and more importantly, to do the things you really love!

Do not get stuck worrying about money in retirement!

Downsizing your existing home is just one of many alternatives you will be able to consider as you plan your golden years!

*****

CHAPTER 23

MUTUAL FUNDS

Formally, a mutual fund is generally a type of professionally managed collective investment fund or vehicle, pooling the funds of many investors to purchase securities.

There is no legal definition of the term "mutual fund." It is most used to describe collective investment vehicles that are regulated (by the SEC) and sold to the public.

In the U.S. there are 3 types: open-end, unit investment trusts, and closed-end funds. Open-end is most common. This means that the fund must be willing to buy back shares from investors every business day. Exchange-traded funds (or "ETFs" for short) are open-ended funds (or unit investment trusts) that trade on a stock exchange just like any other stock, e.g., Apple (AAPL).

Recently, ETFs have been gaining in popularity, mainly because of lower management fees. These fees are generally referred to as the Management Expense Ratio (or "MER") – i.e., the fees an investor would pay a fund manager to expertly manage the fund, regardless of the fund's performance.

Investors pay the fund's expenses, which reduces the fund's returns and/or performance. There is controversy about the level of these expenses because several mutual funds consistently under-perform the S&P 500, Dow, or other indices, while collecting relatively high fees from the investors, regardless of the fund's performance.

Mutual funds are generally classified by their principal investments. The four main categories of funds are money market funds, bond or fixed income funds, stock or equity funds, and hybrid funds.

I opened this chapter, leading off with the word "formally" for a specific reason: Informally, mutual funds and ETFs (albeit perhaps to a lesser degree), are the investment vehicles of choice utilized almost exclusively by the working, middle-class and/or less sophisticated investors.

Large diversification – which is common with mutual funds – does not protect investors from sharp declines in the market. A mutual fund that includes e.g., 20 companies is still *in the market*! Large downturns in the stock market, such as the ones experienced in 1999 or 2009, affect the whole market, including mutual funds... if every single stock in the fund goes down, the mutual fund goes down too.

Also keep in mind that a basic market rule is that downturns happen more sharply than upswings. This means you get slow upside growth and rapid downside losses.

Many working people contribute to a 401k or similar type retirement savings plan. These savings plans generally only allow employees to select one (or a basket) of mutual funds and/or bonds, as may be made available by the carrier (vendor providing the 401k plan administration services). Typically, investment returns fall short of general market returns – as mentioned above – in addition to the investment being subject to (often high) fees.

Simple, common-sense rules for smaller investors may be to:

1. Invest in mutual funds in a 401k plan – to ensure that you

save for your own retirement, and perhaps benefit from employer contributions, or better...

2.   Invest in ETFs instead of mutual funds – if available – because ETF fees are generally much lower than mutual fund
MERs, or even better still...

3.   Create your own basket of stocks (e.g., copy a mutual
fund prospectus, or Buffett's equity holdings) and buy small
quantities of these stocks on a regular basis (to benefit from
cost averaging, as the market goes up and down). The
reason why this may be deemed a better choice is because
one can buy stock via an online brokerage account for minimal cost, with no further, future, downstream management fees.

Whatever choice you make, be sure to capitalize on your employer contribution – if available – because it is free money. More
importantly, make sure you save for your retirement because
your government cannot be trusted to provide for you in the future when you are ready to retire and/or perhaps no longer able
to work.

*****

CHAPTER 24

MUTUAL FUNDS, EPIC FAIL

The mutual fund industry, reliant on unsophisticated and financially illiterate investors, just keeps chugging along without a care in the world.

And why should they care?

After all, employees keep dumping their savings into their products, hoping to save for a grand retirement, ideally aged 65-67, or thereabouts.

What a sad situation!

Let us explore some high-level facts:

1. "Mutual funds are managed by expert, licensed, investment professionals."

While "expert" may be true for the guy at the top of the pyramid, it is only half-true for everyone else responsible for investing… aka taking… as much of your hard-earned cash as possible. They are all obviously licensed… and "investment professionals" is a debatable designation.

Generally, the expert guy (yes, it is usually a guy, and yes, he's been raking in fees for his employer for a long time) at the top of the food chain has achieved outstanding returns in terms of fees generated for his employer. A required, and a primary, expert skill. That is, expertly managing and raking in fees for the company he works for, while expertly delivering some ideally positive returns, to the simple and poor saver, who is diligently contributing to his or her 401k.

While it is true and possible – occasionally – that mutual fund 'investors' achieve a nice return, most of the time the mutual fund under-performs the stock market. But you may say, my mutual fund is invested in blue-chip stocks, like Apple, Google, Microsoft, etc. That is true as well, and the difference in the returns achieved by these companies and the investment return on your mutual fund portfolio was gobbled up by your Mutual Fund Company and its employees. The fees are generally referred to as the MER, which stands for Management Expense Ratio.

2. "Mutual Funds are managed, that's why they charge me a fee. It makes me feel safer, knowing I have a professional managing my portfolio."

Not really, mutual funds are required to publish a prospectus, showing investors exactly what/where they invest contributions into, for example as per the equities mentioned above.

Most mutual fund companies are fabulously inefficient and/or slow (or both) when it comes to managing the investments in their prospectus (i.e., your portfolio). They mostly just buy and hold good stocks. That is why, when the stock market tanked in 2008/9, mutual funds tanked along with the stock market, because that is where they invest!

You could simply copy the top-10 investments in their published prospectus, thereby building your own index of funds, cherry-picked by their "professional and expert team of advisors."

3. "Mutual funds simplify my investment choices and mitigate my investment risk."

What rubbish! Simplify? Yes. Mitigate risk? Absolutely not!

Firstly, saving for your retirement is a good thing, because government hand-outs are rapidly becoming a thing of the past. The problem is more mathematical (or actuarial to be more specific) than political, mainly because people are living longer. The social systems - in place since the 50's - were designed along the same lines as any insurance company's business model: "contributions of many people pay for distributions to few."

I am not advocating that you stop making contributions to your 401k!

In fact, quite the opposite is desirable. You should maximize your contributions to maximize your employer contributions. If your employer's 401k plan administrator only offers a basket of mutual funds to select from, you should still maximize your contributions to receive the employer match, assuming one is available.

The generally poor returns and fees attached to your mutual fund choices will be topped-up by the additional money from your employer... possibly delivering a more competitive, market-related performance for your investment, overall.

Outside of your 401k, first get rid of debt (especially expensive, short-term loans like credit cards) and then stay away from mutual funds. Invest in ETFs (a similar investment to a mutual fund, but lower fees), or ideally... build your own index of good quality equities and hold these investments while reinvesting dividends!

RUDI BESTER

*****

CHAPTER 25

SHOULD RETIREES BUY STOCKS?

Part one

Retirees generally tend to migrate to 'lower risk' investment options e.g., bonds, certified deposit- and/or 'high-yield' savings accounts.

Money in the bank is probably the worst investment choice, even worse than the much higher risk of e.g. investing in that same bank's stock. Instead of putting your money into the bank's savings account... you should rather consider buying the bank's stock!

By way of an example, at the time of writing, the Bank of America ($BAC) Platinum Money Market Savings Account offered an annual percentage yield (interest rate earned) of 0.12% on balances of between $20,000-30,000.

During the 2008/9 financial crisis, Bank of America's stock lost nearly 90% of its value.

If $BAC were an outlier, we can look at one of their peers. A 'more stable one' and one of the best-managed banks in the world - J.P.

Morgan Chase ($JPM) - which is also America's largest bank:

A Chase Plus Savings account offers 0.20% on balances between $25,000 and $50,000. However, in the early 2000's the savings account rates were higher, so - for the sake of this example - we can average the savings account interest rate at 1%.

$30,000 invested at 1% over 10 years compounded (meaning you earn interest also on your interest, every year), would be worth $33,138, for a gain (return on investment) of $3,138.

According to YCharts, in March 2003, JP Morgan stock was valued at $18.56/share. $30,000 would have allowed you to snag about 1,616 shares.

Today (April 2020) JP Morgan stock closed at nearly $100/share, meaning that 1,616 shares would be worth $161,000 (with re-invested dividends) – i.e., more than 5x the original investment.

But you may ask "What if I had picked $BAC instead of $JPM? I may have lost money". Yes, that might have been possible. And yes, you could pick 'the wrong' stock, much like you could pick the wrong mutual fund, bond... or leave your money in a savings account!

A better solution would have been to diversify and pick e.g., 3 banks, like now 'uber conservative' Wells Fargo, 'middle of the conservative range' J.P. Morgan, and 'flying too close to the sun' Bank of America.

Even better may have been to diversify even further and select a couple of blue-chip heavyweights (see part 2) that have traditionally delivered a good return. That way one could complement the bank stocks above with, for example, Johnson & Johnson, and Chevron.

Still nervous? Add three more, across different industries once more, like Caterpillar, Home Depot and Walmart. For good measure (and further risk mitigation), add another, e.g., 3M

Co., and you would have successfully built your own *bulletproof* index of a few Dow Jones Industrial Index (or "Dow") stocks.

Together, these should provide enough risk mitigation, and reasonable returns, allowing you to top the rate on a savings account by >5% annually, without burdening yourself with too much stress. Just do not panic and start selling your stocks when they go down a little!

"Should Retirees Buy Stocks (part 2 below) offers a short analysis and an example that may help retirees select a Dow stock for investment. When you read the information provided, do not fret too much if I have used financial terms that you do not understand – the Dow only includes 30 stocks, so selecting 10 for your own portfolio would not be too much of a challenge.

Note that all the companies mentioned in this post are Dow stocks. This index of 30 stocks is regarded as a leading market indicator, referred to daily as 'the market' ("the market was up/down 20 points today" means the Dow was up/down 20 points). Multi-billion-dollar, American blue-chip companies that have stood the test of time... quite often, much better so than your local bank, that may not even still be in existence today.

The Dow index has historically returned, on average, about 6.8% annually for over 100 years. With reinvested dividends, the Dow returns nearly 10% annually, assuming you can reinvest your dividends earned.

*****

Part Two

Retirees typically invest in low returning investment choices based on the advice of their financial planner, or simply because they may perceive bonds and guaranteed/certified deposit accounts as more safe and secure.

They often invest in these investment vehicles while unfortunately watching the value of their investment portfolios decline faster than their life expectancy. The question begs... where will seniors be able to derive more income from their investments, while at the same time, mitigate the risk of investment losses?

I suppose, if the question were "should I **buy stocks**", the underlying question becomes "how do I choose a stock to invest in?"

For the purposes of this summary, I have elected to use Travelers ($TRV) as an example of a Dow stock that may be suitable for inclusion in a retiree's portfolio.

At a high level, and without getting overly technical, retirees can consider these 5 factors when deciding whether to invest:

1. Size: Ideally, there is safety in relative size and retirees should not be taking chances with new or unproven businesses. TRV is a Dow-Index listed company with a 150-year history as a leading U.S. insurance corporation. The corporation has a market value (or capitalization) of about $39 billion (September 2021) and employs more than 30,000 employees. While large companies may not grow as fast as small companies, large companies offer far greater security than new upstarts.

2. Dividends: Retirees would generally want to earn income via dividends. In addition to healthy payouts now, they should also look for dividend growth over time. TRV offers a current dividend yield of 2.25% (vs. an industry average of 1.23%), a 5-year dividend growth of nearly 10% and 8 consecutive years of dividend increases. Not the greatest, but good.

3. Valuation: For publicly traded corporations, we typically look for a 'normalized' Price/Earnings ratio (P/E = the share

price divided by the earnings per share) of <15. On September 12, 2021, TRV's P/E was 10.5.

4.   Stock Stability: This may be a little too technical, but it is worth sharing anyway for those who are interested. To measure stability, we determine beta, defined as the measure of the risk or volatility of TRV vs. the market. Financial advisors may be looking for a beta of less than 1. A beta of 1 indicates that the security's price will move with the market. Less than 1 means that the security will be less volatile than the market. And greater than 1 indicates that the security's price will be more volatile than the market. For example, if a stock's beta is 1.2, it's theoretically 20% more volatile than the market. Generally, TRV offers a beta of <1, meaning that TRV stock is less volatile than the market. In addition, investors do not like stocks that have experienced losses of greater than e.g., 20% at any time during the past five years. TRV lost only 5.9% in 2008/9 when the stock market 'crashed', faring far better than most other companies.

5.   Consistency: Here we should look at revenue growth – after all, we do not want to invest in a declining company – and specifically at the revenue growth over a period, e.g., 5 years. TRV has generated positive revenue growth for the last 4, and this is acceptable. Another way to analyze consistency would be to explore $TRV free cash flow growth, once again looking for growth over a period of e.g., 5 years. TRV has only managed growth in free cash flow for 2 of the past five years, but as an insurance company, TRV took some heavy body blows because of natural disasters, like hurricanes. Not the greatest in generating free cash flow growth, but respectable. Losses were more because of uncontrollable business events caused by natural disasters (the large insurance payouts), than poor management decisions.

An analysis like the one above is meant to provide highlights of company performance to assist small investors with investment decisions. Your financial advisor would obviously be more in tune with your unique, personal financial situation and investment return requirements.

If you – as a retiree – have most of your wealth invested in a portfolio of relatively poor performing, 'low risk' investment vehicles, speak to your wealth manager to discuss your investment returns achieved. Ensure that you are not invested in a real declining asset portfolio, especially when adjusted for annual inflation!

*****

CHAPTER 26

MACRO-ECONOMIC BUBBLES POPPING

By now, every person on the planet already knows about the 2008/09 housing bubble that effectively eliminated middle-class "wealth" in the United States and most other developed nations.

The 2020 coronavirus pandemic - for most of our younger people, like Millennials - probably represents their second experience or familiarity with an economic reset of large impact.

Their parents, many who would self-describe as baby-boomers, would have seen a few more. Like the 2000 "dot com" crash. Or "Black Monday" in 1987, when the Dow lost more than 20% in one day.

These are some of the reasons why people are so fearful of stock-market investing.

I added quotation marks around the word *wealth* above because most of these middle-class citizens did not own the wealth in their residential property in the first place, but only the imaginary gains that would be achieved if the property were sold, less the mortgage owing, or outstanding.

As sellers (assisted by over-zealous realtors) pushed home prices ever higher, combined with a decreased cost of borrowing (e.g., mortgage rates at an all-time low), people kept buying larger and more expensive homes - certainly paying more than the replacement cost of the house by far - and living beyond their means.

Today, if the outstanding mortgage is greater than the possible sales price of the house - as is the case for many homeowners across America - we refer to them as being underwater.

However, there are two more bubbles that will cause future corrections in the near- to medium term.

These are:

1. Student debt

American and Canadian parents (and parents from other countries also, but I can only comment on what I know), have been indoctrinated to believe that their children are entitled to a college education.

This is regardless of the often-dire personal financial situation of the parents.

Many parents - well intended, no doubt - had used Home Equity Lines of Credit (HELOCs) to help fund the cost of education for their children, helping to exacerbate the situation described above.

Using their residential property as an ABM, they kept borrowing against the fictitious future resale value, feeling confident in their poor financial/lifestyle choice for two hopelessly incorrect reasons:

(a) the value of their home will keep going up, and

(b) their kids will not be able to get good jobs without a college degree

Now, as U.S. unpaid student loans exceed $1 trillion, these young graduates cannot afford to repay their debt.

This is mainly because they cannot get work commensurate with their unrealistic expectations (or entitlements) as a college graduate, inclusive of a salary high enough to allow them to repay the debt.

Many young graduates work in retail for minimum wage because that is the only job they are able to get hired for.

Even worse, the parents are often saddled with the first mortgage, a second one, a HELOC, and an adult child back at home who cannot find good employment!

The government - mismanaging federal student loan programs just as badly as they mismanage other social programs - offer debt forgiveness, refinancing, etc. to students who would perhaps have been better off without the debt (sometimes $200,000) and their worthless college degree!

How will this situation end?

Regrettably, not well... and the summary above only scratches the surface of a growing financial burden and future bubble, ready to pop!

2. Property tax

You might have seen a few media reports about a housing recovery.

If you believe those, or bluster from politicians during election campaigns, then you are in for a rude awakening.

One primary reason why many resale properties (and new, but perhaps to a lesser degree) cannot sell is because of ever increasing, burgeoning, property tax.

Property tax on a residential home is no longer related to the real value, property size or acreage, number of rooms, street frontage, etc.

Property tax may be mathematically based on some combination of these factors - i.e. if your neighbor's house is larger, she may pay more tax, pro-rated - but the actual gross amount of the tax, or the total due each year, is required as a contribution to your local government's unaffordable compensation schemes, pensions to support retired workers, and some of the cost required to fund services (like schools, roads, etc.).

In fact, if you were to take the time and trouble to review, even at a high level, your local town's budget, you will be amazed to see most of your property taxes are being allocated towards compensation (salaries, pensions).

This next bubble is already in existence, a problem that will be exacerbated by falling property prices in the future, because the price ebbs and flows are cyclical.

With the low cost of borrowing, every $100,000 of mortgage debt costs the average person with reasonably good credit less than $500/month. That means that a $200,000 mortgage would cost the borrower less than $1,000/month.

This sum may be considered affordable to most middle-class Americans.

However, the property tax for residential homes in states like New Jersey, New York, and Connecticut (that I'm most familiar with) often exceed the cost of borrowing for the required mortgage.

For example, if the property tax on a house in these 'bankrupt states' runs at $12,000 annually (a common scenario), the potential buyer is faced with a dilemma: while the $1,000/month mortgage payment may have been affordable, the additional $1,000/month makes the total cost of ownership unaffordable (especially considering utilities, insurance, ongoing maintenance, etc.).

The result is twofold: (1) people who may have aspired to home ownership - regardless of the reason - keep renting and (2) local governments under ever increasing pressure to fund and support the union demands of their existing and retired employees, have ongoing downward pressure on their incoming revenue (as owners default, file for tax value re-adjustments, leave the town, etc.), with ever increasing costs (higher pensions and medical insurance for retired employees; higher wages and benefits for current employees).

So... what happens now?

Some towns and some homeowners file for bankruptcy; a few borrowers refinance and change their ways. The next bubble? You bet... the cost of funding government in its current state is simply unsustainable.

The fix is simple... buy what you can afford, based on your family requirements, and NOT to impress your family, colleagues and/ or friends.

It is the most fundamental rule of all financial literacy: Live within your means!

*****

Made in the USA
Columbia, SC
05 March 2023

13157755R00161